The Customer Mindset

THE CUSTOMER MINDSET

**THINKING LIKE YOUR CUSTOMER TO
CREATE REMARKABLE RESULTS**

Joe DeRosa

Copyright © 2016 Joe DeRosa
All rights reserved.

ISBN: 153301096X
ISBN 13: 9781533010964

Table of Contents

Preface · vii

Chapter 1   Begin at the Beginning · 1

Chapter 2   The Hazards of Not Listening · · · · · · · · · · · · · · · · 6

Chapter 3   Everything Begins with a Need · · · · · · · · · · · · · · · 11

Chapter 4   Vision and Its Role in the Buyer's Journey · · · · · · · · · · 20

Chapter 5   The Art of the Customer Interview · · · · · · · · · · · · · · 25

Chapter 6   The Buyer's Journey · 33

Chapter 7   Creating a Buyer's Persona · · · · · · · · · · · · · · · · · · 44

Chapter 8   Disrupting the Market · 48

Chapter 9   Establishing Your Market Position · · · · · · · · · · · · · · 53

Chapter 10   A Few Words On Pricing · · · · · · · · · · · · · · · · · · · 59

Chapter 11   Getting the Right People on the Bus · · · · · · · · · · · · 64

Chapter 12   The Power of "So What" · 68

Chapter 13   Putting Things in Motion · 71

Chapter 14   The Role of Social Media in the Buyer's Journey · · · · · · 75

Chapter 15   Developing Your Content Strategy · · · · · · · · · · · · · · · · · 86

Chapter 16   A Final Word on the Buyer's Journey · · · · · · · · · · · · · · · 99

             Acknowledgments · 101

Preface

Curiosity is the precursor to all inventions and innovations. Wondering why, dreaming, brainstorming, or simply thinking about why things are the way they are have always interested me. I've never been one to accept the position "just because." Given my curious predisposition, it's no surprise I have been drawn to a career that requires curiosity, creativity, and vision.

I started selling when I was thirteen years old. My cousin and I started a lawn-cutting business in which our target customers were older, widowed women who couldn't cut their lawns for themselves or afford to pay a regular lawn service. We would charge seven or eight dollars to cut a half-acre lot that took us about forty-five minutes to complete. We felt like kings making three to four dollars in cash per hour. In our first summer, we had six customers we would cut grass for weekly, and our customer base grew to two dozen weekly customers after ten years. More than thirty years later, as I look back, I realize that my interest in the buyer's journey started when I was a kid. I was fascinated by what caused a buyer to take action—to buy, or not to buy. The key was providing a great service at a reasonable price. It was as a teenager that I started giving thought to the balance between the price a buyer is willing to pay versus the benefit that buyer receives; today I call this balance the value equation.

I kept that lawn-cutting business for ten years and kept it going for the last five of those years on my own. I did this while going to college full time and working a number of jobs from retail to fast food. My big break came in 1987 when I was hired to sell ATM cards over the phone for First Federal Savings and Loan of Rochester (now part of HSBC Bank). Imagine cutting your teeth in your first sales job on a product no one knows about, no one wants, and everyone is skeptical of. I got very comfortable, very quickly, with using the phone as a sales tool. It was by far the best experience I could have asked for to prepare me for a career focused on serving buyers.

Over the past twenty years, I have held a number of senior leadership positions with many Fortune 500 companies, as well as some venture-backed firms. I've had complete responsibility for generating top-line revenue for companies operating in the financial services space, as well as business services, professional services, and insurance. I have gathered years of experience, and data, surrounding the revenue funnel, which starts with brand awareness and ends with fulfillment (ringing the cash register).

Beginning in 2005, I found my passion for studying and understanding what buyers go through prior to arriving at a decision to purchase a product or service. I wondered if there were similarities in buying behaviors from business-to-business, business-to-consumer, and business-to-business-to-consumer channels. I wanted to understand if the decision-making process changed when a buyer purchased something for individual use versus a purchase made on behalf of a business. I took every opportunity I could to get exposure to different types of buyers, including consumers and businesses. I participated in a host of advisory councils, workshops, and focus groups, all designed and executed with the intent to better explain what drives buyer behavior. That same year, I developed a process that I would use, and continue to refine, which provides a roadmap for conducting work on the buyer's journey. Since then I have met (face-to-face) with thousands of customers and potential buyers. I have isolated key moments of truth along the buyer's journey—steps in the journey that the buyer perceives to be more important than other steps.

I have introduced this approach to a number of companies where I have held executive leadership roles and have seen firsthand the benefits and challenges of this work. On the benefits side, I have participated in great successes that I'd place into the following four categories:

1. Collaboration

When an organization commits to understanding the needs of its buyers, it creates a culture of curiosity and collaboration. Team members begin to wonder, ask why, and challenge the status quo. Conversations that begin with "what if" begin to fill the company's hallways, cubicles, offices, and conference rooms. These conversations plant the seeds for ideation that begin to sprout up across many different functional areas of the business. The team rallies around, creating a remarkable experience for the customer. Honest dialogue begins to take shape up and down the chain of command, getting leaders involved in the details while those producing the details begin getting involved in strategy. Collaboration becomes the tie that binds.

2. Product Improvements

Understanding the buyer's needs and behaviors as they relate to the actual usage of your product is critical when developing product enhancements. Creating a simple integration between payroll data and QuickBooks is one example, and developing a six-question online insurance application providing an instant quote to the buyer is another in the product improvements I have participated in as a result of conducting buyer-journey work. Having this outside-in view from the buyer's viewpoint minimizes the chances that the wrong changes will be made, including changes that provide little to no value to the buyer.

3. Service Improvements

Conversations with your buyers will deliver some of the richest insights and perspectives imaginable. Often what's learned through these interactions highlights the importance of the buyer's emotions in the buying process. How many calls it took to get a question answered, or problem resolved, can be quite instructive in addressing current service procedures. Likewise, the hold times, the number of transfers, or the incorrect answers that failed to answer the buyer's questions or resolve the buyer's problem will also shed light on areas in your service process that require improvements. Using what I've learned from doing buyer-journey work has led to the creation of a customer care center and to launching a dedicated customer service model in which a group of customers are serviced by a dedicated representative.

4. Marketing and Sales Improvements

Last, but certainly not least, are the improvements that can be made to your marketing and sales strategies that result from understanding your buyer's journey. What to say, how to say it, when to say it, and where to say it are all key inputs that go into creating a message that resonates with your buyer. But it doesn't stop with the right message. There are countless examples of great products with brilliant messaging that fail to sell. Until recently, within the last five to six years, the sales team operated completely independently from the marketing team. Sales had its own process that it developed to "sell" the buyer. With the advent of sales enablement, companies now have a secret weapon in bringing these two functions together in order to best maximize each buyer interaction. The buyer's journey informs both the messaging and the sales process used to interact with the buyer.

One might think that with all the benefits that result from learning about your buyer's journey that there would be few obstacles in conducting this critically needed work. Yet obstacles do exist. In fact, I have found that some of the greatest challenges in commencing a buyer-journey engagement are more the result of internal squabbles or disagreements than challenges originating with the buyer. I have observed three common obstacles to conducting formal buyer-journey work that originate within executive leadership teams:

1. Denial

Many leaders operate in complete denial of their circumstances. I've seen heated and intense arguments ensue over the mere thought that the business was not performing at its best. Even in situations in which the company's actual financial results seemed to demand a change in strategy, many leaders were still reluctant to believe things were as bad as they were. They refused to believe their strategy was incorrect or that they didn't have the right talent to execute it. In the worst-case scenarios, I've seen leaders bring down a business all in the name of protecting a chosen few. They became fixated on the possible findings the buyer's journey would uncover and how those findings might affect those they were trying hardest to protect. As a result, they tended to stonewall this important work.

2. Lack of trust

Trust is also a major challenge to conducting buyer-journey work. Leaders need to trust the colleagues conducting this work as much as they trust the feedback the buyer provides. Establishing trust throughout the entire organization, regardless of size, is paramount in conducting buyer-journey mapping. Keep in mind the number-one reason for commencing buyer-journey work is to make the buyer's experience so remarkable that he or she will not only buy from you once, but again, and again, and again. The number-two reason you're doing this work is to convert the buyer into a raving fan who speaks so beautifully about you and your business to friends and family that you begin to receive customer referrals. There are no other reasons to embark on this type of work. It all begins—and ends—with the customer.

3. Lack of courage

Finally, a likely byproduct of lack of trust is a leader's lack of courage. Some leaders are simply afraid. They are afraid to be wrong, afraid to take action, afraid to make a mistake, or afraid to be seen as someone lacking all the answers. It's difficult to have the courage to take action if you lack the trust of those who are suggesting, directing, or proposing the action. Look for executive sponsorship from a leader who has courage. A leader who genuinely believes in the customer, and providing the customer with a remarkable experience, is the most likely ally in commencing this work.

The purpose of this book is to provide key insights into how to actively engage your buyers to deliver sustainable revenue growth. This is not pie-in-the-sky stuff. It's not a moon shot, a fairy tale, or a naive view of the business world. There are tangible benefits from doing this work. I will provide a number of examples of innovations that have been made resulting from this work, as well as examples of failures from not understanding the buyer's needs. This work is challenging work, no doubt. It's not easy, but it's also not impossible. I will present a framework and path forward that will help you take control of getting to the bottom of your buyer's journey. Over the course of my twenty-year career, I've gathered deep customer insights and will present realistic methods and tactics that can be applied to any business to help you do the same. Stay focused on the benefits of this work while keeping in tune with the challenges that may arise. The benefits of understanding your buyer's journey are invaluable. From establishing goodwill to developing new ways to serve the customer in a manner that delights, this work is quite fulfilling. Solving problems, easing pain, removing burdens, and creating peace of mind are all benefits of gaining insight into your buyer's journey.

I have been blessed to have learned so much from the customers I have served throughout my career. Simply by taking the time to care, to ask for their opinions and ideas, and to be vulnerable in a way that provided them with unfiltered insight into my opportunities, challenges, dilemmas, and innovations, I have developed hundreds of lifelong relationships I can still count on when I need to test my thinking. If you're willing to be curious, willing to ask questions, and willing to be open-minded, there is no limit to the insights and experience you will gain from understanding your buyer's journey.

CHAPTER 1

BEGIN AT THE BEGINNING

The beginning is the most important part of the work.
—*Plato*

Every life has a beginning and an end. All living things are born, grow, and ultimately die. Along life's journey there are starts, stops, stumbles, and revivals. Businesses are no different; they begin with an idea. Someone is daring enough to take a chance to develop and deliver an idea into the market in exchange for some form of payment. From there the business grows. It experiences obstacles, stumbles, restarts, fails, and may ultimately go out of business. This is a natural life cycle for business. But why do some businesses succeed while others fail? Why are some businesses able to restart or revive and still others stall and die?

It doesn't matter if you're talking about Amazon, BlackBerry, IBM, Intuit, RCA, Tesla, or countless other companies; each got its start from a brilliant invention or innovation. And while some of these companies are widely considered successful in 2016, the fact is that others are not, and still others have encountered their share of challenges and "near misses."

In his memoir, *Who Says Elephants Can't Dance,* Lou Gerstner talks about the turnaround of IBM, one of America's most storied companies. One of the greatest inventors in history, Thomas Watson, founded

International Business Machines in 1911. By the late 1980s, into the early 1990s, IBM was struggling, having strayed from its core business. The result? Upset customers, lost revenue, and a crisis of confidence. What Gerstner did immediately upon landing the top job at IBM was to meet with, and talk to, dozens of the company's top customers. These deep conversations provided the insights that Gerstner needed to chart a course to regain the confidence IBM had previously lost with its customers, employees, and other stakeholders. Gerstner did not let fear prevent him from engaging his customers. In fact, he embraced that engagement, knowing full well that much of what he would soon learn about his company would not be flattering or pleasant. Nonetheless, he dove headfirst into his buyers' journeys.

Over time, our skills and intuitions become dulled as we drink more and more of the corporate Kool-Aid. We begin to believe that we actually know more about what our customers need than they themselves do. We stop asking. We stop being curious. We stop being innovative. We stop being comfortable with being uncomfortable. We settle in. Actually, we just settle. We develop stories that provide excuses for our current circumstances. These stories explain why we're not selling as much as we want to, why our customers aren't buying, and how our competitors are playing unfairly.

Today's marketplace is a highly complex organism. It lives, breathes, adapts, and evolves every minute of every day, every week, and every year. The process is nonstop. World events such as terrorism, economic turmoil, cyber threats, and famines create obstacles that the marketplace adjusts to and moves beyond. Leaders, of both countries and companies, are paid to maintain a finger on the pulse of these events and provide vision and solutions that successfully navigate these matters. A leader's confidence and conviction are paramount to his or her effectiveness in dealing with challenging circumstances. Likewise, the leader's experience provides the depth needed to foresee potential pitfalls and adjust accordingly to avoid or minimize them altogether.

Leaders are charged with providing the vision, or what I call the destination postcard.

Where is it you're ultimately trying to go? What will it look like when you arrive? How long will it take? What's involved with getting there?

These questions, and others like them, are asked regularly by senior leadership teams, boards, investors, and, yes, your customers. As a leader you will be responsible for answering them. Your followers need to know. They have a right to know. You will at times feel validated, challenged, supported, and perhaps even vindicated, depending on your circumstances. Regardless, you will most certainly experience a time when your answer to these questions is met with strong resistance, denial, or, worse, a loss of confidence. No matter, you own it. Having quantitative and qualitative customer insights that support your vision, recommendations, and plans will provide some level of validation. Yet even with mountains of data, key stakeholders may still push back or reject your thinking. If you reach this point after taking all the right steps presented in this book, and still cannot garner executive-level support to effect a needed change to improve the buyer's experience, then my coaching to you would be to begin thinking about moving on. Rarely does bad news get better with time, and just as rare are epiphany moments within the C-Suite (Senior executives with titles that start with the letter C, for chief executive officer, chief operations officer, etc). If you feel deeply passionate about being a customer advocate, and you're trapped in a company that resists change, I'd describe your journey as being on the highway to hell. While you may be able to tolerate a disconnect between your values and the company's for a little while, you won't be able to sustain a disconnect forever. If you do, you've settled. And don't be fooled into thinking you're the only one who knows you've settled. Your team sees it, and so do your customers. It begins to tear away at any confidence they have in your ability to effect change.

Once a leader suffers a loss of confidence, that leader may as well stay home. Whether the loss of confidence is from the board, the chief executive officer, the team, or the customer, the leader is now rendered ineffective. Without confidence among the stakeholders, there can be no alignment in strategy. Settling, or going with the flow, may feel like the safe thing to do at the moment, but understand that, ultimately, inaction will most likely result in a crisis of confidence. When the confidence is gone, so too will be the leader.

I've had the pleasure of serving in several senior executive roles at a number of different companies. Firsthand, I have seen companies that live innovation versus those that simply use innovation as a motto or corporate platitude. I've worked for leaders who have inspired me, pushed me, challenged me, developed me, and invested in me. These are the most authentic of authentic leaders. They "do" because the result of developing people around them adds a priceless amount of value to the organization. At the same time, I've worked for a number of people who held the title of leader but who in fact were not leaders at all. Instead, they worried primarily about themselves, not making waves, and paying attention to the public opinion polls. They had little vision, little courage, and little contribution to the development of other organizational leaders and, perhaps coincidentally, had no interest in understanding the buyer's experience. In some cases the organization rid itself of these ineffective leaders, and in other cases it eliminated the entire team, all because there was no confidence in the leader.

The great leaders showed me the value of courage. They showed me the difference between doing things right versus doing the right things; and why both are important. They taught me the significance of developing those around me: servant leadership. This extends beyond your direct reports and carries over to your customers as well. Chick-fil-A asks every customer who arrives: "How may I serve you?" Employees don't ask how they can help. They view their purpose as something deeper than helping. They exist to serve. That's a belief that cascades from founder S. Truett Cathy on down.

With vision comes the ability and confidence to begin at the beginning. A leader should strive to maintain a beginner's mind-set. If I had to start this today, how would I do it? What would it look like? How would I structure it? A leader should not be afraid to suggest or make a change even if it reverses a strategy or direction he or she previously set. A leader has the express responsibility to his followers to be constantly evaluating and assessing his current position and the variables that can have a positive or negative effect on the organization's progress to achieving its goals.

CHAPTER 2

THE HAZARDS OF NOT LISTENING

The world is moving, and a company that contents itself with present accomplishments soon falls behind.
—GEORGE EASTMAN

The year was 1892, and the United States was bustling with history-making activity. Benjamin Harrison, the president of the United States, would soon lose his reelection to Grover Cleveland, the only US president to ever serve two nonconsecutive terms. Ellis Island had just begun to take its first arrival of immigrants into the country on January 1, 1892 and the Pledge of Allegiance was first recited in unison in public schools on October 12, 1892.

The business climate had been stable leading up to 1892, and that stability was partially led by the rise of agricultural products made in the United States and shipped abroad, specifically throughout Europe. The country's unemployment rate was estimated at 3 percent—quite low by standards for that time period. But things were about to get bumpy. The Reading Railroad was on the cusp of failure as the result of two factors: the government's desire to break up monopolies, and steps taken by J.P. Morgan, Reading's primary financial backer, in pulling the plug on Reading's credit. At the same time these developments were unfolding, Europe's economy began to contract, becoming the harbinger for the Panic of 1893. Yet in the midst of all this instability, a little-known thirty-nine-year-old from Waterville, New York, was busy founding what would become one of the most iconic companies of our age. His name was George Eastman.

In 1884, George Eastman patented the first rolled film. By 1888 he had invented the first camera designed specifically to be used with rolled film. Eastman's innovation popularized film, bringing picture-taking into the mainstream. Later that year, rolled film was credited with providing the basis for the invention of motion picture film, leading George Eastman, riding a wave of popularity, to launch Kodak in Rochester, New York.

By 1976, Kodak, the film and camera leader, commanded a 90 percent market share of all film sales and 80 percent of camera sales. The company generated $16 billion in revenue, had more than fifteen thousand employees, and was ranked the fifth most valuable brand in the world, according to the *Harvard Business Review*.

As a child growing up in Kodak's hometown of Rochester, New York, I knew the importance of this company on a personal level. Many of my aunts, uncles, cousins, and friends called Kodak home. And while I had no idea, or comprehension, of its business contributions relative to paying taxes, innovation, or market dominance, I felt proud taking out my Kodak Instamatic to snap pictures. Yet by 2015 this once-iconic company that created the *Kodak Moment* had dwindled to sixty-five hundred employees generating approximately $1.31 billion in revenue. So what happened? The simple answer is that the company wasn't listening.

Businesses large and small go through a natural life cycle. In his book for leaders in transition, *The First 90 Days*, Michael Watkins outlines these stages with his business life-cycle model he refers to as STARS: startup, turnaround, realignment, and sustaining success. Some companies fit squarely into one category while others may straddle more than one stage simultaneously. There are other models that also provide insight into the business life cycle, with subtle variations. What they all have in common is a beginning and end. Where they vary is what falls between those two bookends.

Photo by Ivan Sabo

From the time a business begins, it is evolving. Like a toddler learning how to walk, new businesses stumble and often fall. In fact, more than 50 percent of all new business starts fail within the first year. So if half fail, the other half may stumble forward, regain their footing, and enjoy success. But even this success is temporary if the business pushes back against its own evolution. The process may look linear, circular, or even like a hopscotch of events. The key is to know exactly where you are, and why you're there, in order to move forward as quickly and effectively as possible. Getting to neutral is one of the most difficult positions for many leaders to grasp. The neutral position is your baseline. It's where you are today. Understanding your baseline requires you to confront reality—something many leaders resist. All too often leaders fall into the trap of making excuses—blaming the customer for the business's challenges and struggles, or believing the organization's plight is tied to the fact (or so the leader believes) that customers will "learn the hard way" by giving their business to a competitor. This demonstration of hubris is not uncommon, and many times it proves fatal.

Kodak's failure was the primary result of its leadership not properly confronting its reality. The trend toward digital had been sparked by none other than Kodak itself. A young inventor named Steven Sasson was hired by the company after graduating from Rensselaer Polytechnic Institute in 1973. Less than two years after joining Kodak, Sasson invented the first digital camera. The original device, invented in 1975, was a hodgepodge of components tied together, including the lens from a Super 8 movie camera, a portable digital tape recorder, nickel-cadmium batteries, and several dozen circuits. The camera was able to take a picture and convert it into a digital format, but it was still not yet able to then convert that format into a visual picture; Sasson still needed to create a converter. Finally, in 1978, Sasson patented the first digital camera, and it was called the electronic still camera. However, his bosses at Kodak refused to let him talk about it. The film giant feared this device would lead to its losing its grip as the leader in photography. Kodak's inability to look down the road and envision the opportunity this digital innovation presented set the company on a destructive path—one that would destroy shareholder value, costs thousands of jobs, and result in a failure of epic proportions. By the way, Kodak is not the only company whose failures and demise were due to some degree of hubris. Some leaders simply are not capable of making difficult choices or decisions. Whether in good times or bad, a leader must always be looking around the corner, preparing for the unexpected. Sometimes executives running (not leading) companies with huge market share and brand recognition develop an air of invincibility—hubris. Once hubris sets in, the executive and the team become ineffective. The executive loses touch with reality. The **team is unable to see things as they are, where it is going, and how it needs to adapt.** The team becomes blind—neutralized—and before long its members are unemployed.

Examples like Kodak shine the light on leadership failures. If the company leadership doesn't make it a priority to get to know the customer and listen to the customer's needs, then who will do it? Who will carry the torch for this very important work? If the leadership isn't leading, no one will. Kodak's leaders stopped asking questions and weren't listening for the clues their customers were providing. They lost their curiosity as they became complacent because of the success of the situation at the time. Their falsely held belief that they were the only game in town cost them dearly. Their customers had more choices than they appeared to be aware of. They got it all wrong simply because they weren't paying attention.

The business highway is littered with examples of companies left on the roadside, passed by others who were more curious, more visionary, and better listeners. Kodak, Blackberry, Nokia, and Circuit City are examples of companies whose executive teams may have lost touch with their buyers. Whether they stopped asking before they stopped listening or they continued to ask but didn't listen is irrelevant. The outcome was the same. Stop listening to what your buyer says is wanted, and soon you'll find yourself in rough waters. Like a ship that loses its rudder, your business will begin to drift, getting knocked around by the waves. Your customers are those waves. Stop asking your buyer about what's needed, and you'll soon find that the buyer has changed so much you have no time to adjust. It all begins with identifying the buyer's needs and the impact each of those needs has on *the buyer's* business.

CHAPTER 3

EVERYTHING BEGINS WITH A NEED

Necessity is the mother of invention.
—*PLATO*

People are driven into action by their needs. The more basic the need, the stronger the action. Throughout history, mankind has gone to great lengths, up to and including war, to satisfy the basic needs of food, water, and shelter. Conflicts from the Middle East to Ireland, Somalia, and Sudan have sprouted up because these basic needs were not met. Food and water are the ultimate necessities of life, and therefore their absence results in some of the most aggressive actions human beings will take.

Wants, on the other hand, also have degrees of importance and volatility, but they are driven primarily by emotion rather than physical well-being. Food, water, and shelter provide physical safety and security and, as such, qualify as needs. A want satisfies an emotion. It's highly unlikely that unfulfilled wanting of an inground pool, a Maserati, a Macbook, or a Sub-Zero refrigerator will result in death. You might be bummed for having to settle for something less, but it's not a life or death situation.

In business you must be able to identify the current pain, or potential pain, your customer feels or will feel in order for your business to thrive. As the buyer's pain increases, so does the speed at which he wants to eliminate that pain. The stronger the pain, the faster the buyer wants it gone. The lesser the pain, the more it becomes a nuisance rather than a critical issue. Buyers live with it, or ignore it, until the pain becomes strong enough that it forces them to take action. Being able to recognize the level of pain is important. To do that, you must be able to separate your buyers' wants from their needs.

Below is an illustration of the *wants and needs* spectrum. Effectively plotting where your customer sits on this spectrum is critical to creating a starting point relative to understanding the depth of the customer's needs.

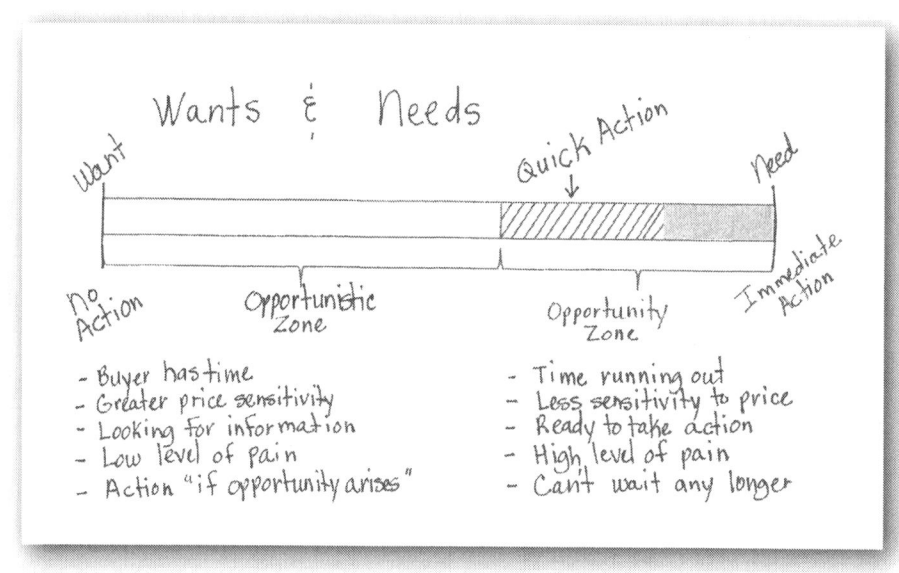

Illustration above by Terri DeRosa

In the illustration above, notice how something that is defined as 100 percent *want* requires no action, while something that is 100 percent *need* must be resolved immediately. To be clear, if you have a *want*, it does not mean you'll never act to fulfill it. It simply means that it will be fulfilled at some point in the future when either the pain becomes more acute or after other personal objectives have been met, allowing for discretionary wants to be addressed. I may want a pair of Ferragamo shoes. I won't get them until I've saved the $700 they cost and my other financial priorities have been met. As you read this, you may be thinking about the people you know who act on their wants before their needs. Sure, that audience exists. But that's not the audience that will build your business. What will help you build your business is understanding where your prospective buyers sit along this spectrum.

The wants and needs spectrum contains two distinct zones:

1. Opportunistic Zone
2. Opportunity Zone

The Opportunistic Zone (the left side of the spectrum) favors wants more than needs. The buyer who is situated in this zone operates with the mind-set of "if the opportunity arises." There is little, if any, pain the buyer experiences in this part of the spectrum.

The Opportunity Zone begins slightly to the right of the midway point on the spectrum—call it 55 percent. Why does the Opportunity Zone begin slightly right of the halfway point on the spectrum? The answer lies in probabilities, and how our brain works to assess preventing potential outcomes from happening.

Recently I read an article written by an individual suffering from chronic pain that arose from a dental mishap. For those who have ever experienced a toothache or any dental problems, you'll know this is some of the worst pain you'll ever experience.

This pain persisted for fourteen years as the patient sought treatment from a number of different doctors, dentists, and oral surgeons. He explained that when meeting with a medical professional, he made his decision as to whether or not he'd proceed with the recommended treatment based on the *probability* of whether it would provide him relief. If the doctor gave a fifty-fifty chance, he would not act. "It simply wasn't enough upside to make me endure yet another procedure, let alone the cost of doing whatever it was they were suggesting I have done"the patient said. He only began considering taking action when the probability was greater than 50 percent.

People take action when they reach a point where they believe they have a stronger chance of that action improving their situation, not before. The key is to understand where on the spectrum your buyer sits as it relates to wants and needs, and more specifically which zone the buyer occupies at the time.

Opportunistic Zone—the *Wants*
Things that fall into the Opportunistic Zone tend to be impulsive or spur of the moment. They are typically closer to a want than a need. You may want a new dress to attend your company's annual holiday party. In August as you're shopping, you find a dress you love, and it's on sale. Your need isn't immediate as the party is still five months away, but the dress is on sale. It's an opportunistic purchase that satisfies a future need while saving money.

In business, an opportunistic need may be acquiring promotional items with your company's logo on them. Another example may be attending an industry conference where you can meet and network with prospective customers. Or perhaps another opportunistic need might involve testing a new mobile application that promotes its ability to improve sales results.

The Opportunistic Zone includes unplanned or impulse purchases and purchases that are specified in a future buying plan unless the opportunity arises sooner. They often carry a high sensitivity to price because the pain has not yet grown to a point where the buyer feels forced to deal with it. Business capital expenditures are an example that may fit within the Opportunistic Zone as they are typically planned and budgeted for in the future. However, if the person tasked with procurement stumbles upon a great deal for new office furniture or new computer equipment, this opportunistic need suddenly becomes an immediate need in order to take advantage of an opportunity to save money.

Since buyers mostly take action in this zone when there is a price savings, you can see the impact price has within the Opportunistic Zone. On December 29, 2014, I happened to take my car into the dealer for normal maintenance. While there, I saw a huge sign proclaiming, "Year-end sales event," and there were rebates, promotions, etc., if you took delivery of the vehicle by December 31. I had been considering getting a new car, but not for another nine to twelve months. It wasn't an immediate need. I fell squarely into the opportunistic zone. As I waited for my car to be serviced, I asked a salesperson about the promotions. As soon as I was able to identify the potential savings by acting sooner rather than later, I asked him to provide me a trade-in value for my car. After some back and forth, I decided to walk. I didn't have to do anything. Remember, I fell 100 percent into the Opportunistic Zone. I had no immediate pain and therefore had no incentive to act unless the price was right. Because I was willing to walk, and knowing that price was the sole driver of my decision, the salesperson quickly came back and provided more money toward my trade. I bought the car and took delivery by two in the afternoon on New Year's Eve! Completely opportunistic.

Opportunity Zone—Quick-Action Needs

A need that requires quick action presents the buyer with a fair amount of pain. There is some discomfort within this zone, and even some recognition from the buyer of an understanding that, if not dealt with soon, the pain will only grow more severe. Quick-action needs are needs that have to be dealt with in order to avoid having them turn into immediate-action needs. Securing health insurance may be a quick-action need. You might not be sick today, but there's a high likelihood that at some point in the near future you'll *need* to see a doctor. Changing your oil regularly is a quick-action need. Once you reach the manufacturer's recommended miles driven, an oil change becomes preventive maintenance, or a quick-action need. Avoiding, delaying, or ignoring a quick-action need will turn it into an immediate need.

In business, a quick-action need may be ordering office supplies or performing maintenance or repairs on a building. It may be securing an umbrella insurance policy or purchasing an extended warranty on a piece of equipment. It may be cleaning a public restroom or shoveling a walkway to the front door. Quick-action needs may also have seasonal connections. Your company may throw a summer picnic every July for its employees. As you begin to plan a year in advance, your need is not immediate but requires quick action in order to secure the venue, caterer, entertainment, etc.

Perhaps you sell event planning to large companies. You know that Salesforce.com, HubSpot, and SiriusDecisions all have major annual conferences or summits that attract thousands of people. Understanding where they are in the process relative to the timeframe for their respective events is critical to gaining insight into where on the wants and needs spectrum they appear. Even though the event may be six, nine, or twelve months into the future, the need falls between a quick-action need and immediate need on the spectrum. This means the customers have time for self-education and shopping around. They don't have an endless runway, but they do have some time, which is another example of the difference between immediate-action need and quick-action needs.

Price becomes less important of a consideration as the buyer travels across the spectrum from the opportunistic zone into the opportunity zone. Why? Because the more severe the pain becomes, the stronger the desire to eliminate it. The closer the buyer gets to a pure need, the less sensitive he or she is to price. When our pain is the most acute, we're willing to spend whatever it takes to eliminate it. It's important to note that while the buyers may be in the opportunity zone, if they are still in the quick-action area, they believe they still have time to shop around before making their decision. The more balanced the value equation is for a quick-action need, the better likelihood you have that the buyer chooses you. The key here is balance—not the cheapest or lowest price. This is where many businesses get confused in setting pricing policy. More on that later. For now, understand that your prospective buyer must see the value and, further, believe in it. The scale for a quick-action need must be slightly tipped in the buyer's favor, but as the buyer moves further toward an immediate need, the scale can actually become level and in some cases tilted in the seller's favor. Since a quick-action need still allows the buyer time to make a decision, the trust and credibility component of the decision-making process is crucial to making the sale.

Opportunity Zone—Immediate Action Needs

The closer the need gets to the right of the spectrum, the more intense the pain and the more essential it is to deal with it. Some needs are so immediate that once we become conscious of the need, we can focus on little else. The need consumes us until it's satisfied or eliminated. Think about it. Have you ever been sitting in a meeting when you were so hungry your stomach was cramping? All of a sudden you begin to tune out. The only thing that matters is satisfying that hunger. Or what about sitting in a concert when the need arises to go to the restroom. It could be the best show, best performance, ever, and you hear nothing. The need to take care of a basic human process overrides all else.

In the business world, an immediate need could be your weekly payroll, collecting your accounts receivable, hiring an employee to fill the role that's been open for months, dealing with a sensitive human resource problem, or getting a line of credit in place to provide the business with needed working capital. These immediate needs can be tied to very specific pain points. If payroll is wrong, you've got unhappy employees. If you can't secure a line of credit for working capital purposes, perhaps you can't fulfill your orders, or, worse, maybe you have to lay off some of your workers. If you let a human resource complaint escalate, you could be placing your business in legal jeopardy.

Immediate needs are the most intense needs we experience. If the solution you offer meets an immediate need, your marketing message should state exactly that. In the payroll business, the focus has always been on peace of mind. Whether it's about paying your employees on time and correctly, or filing your taxes properly so you don't incur penalties, payroll providers solve an immediate need. After all, most people are paid either weekly or every other week, and taxes are collected each pay period and filed quarterly. Fairly immediate. Information technology support is another area that requires meeting an immediate need. When systems go down, or run slow, it impacts business. The need to fix the problem is now; it's immediate.

Immediate needs can involve a commodity all the way to a highly complex, or unique, solution. The need for heating oil can be as immediate as the need to secure a customer relationship management system to provide insight into where sales and service employees are spending their time, and what the return on investment is on that time. Public relations assistance can also become an immediate need. In fact, by its very definition, public relations and its activities are always immediate; they are dealing with something sensitive in nature, whether it's great news that needs to be shared quickly or bad news that needs to be managed effectively.

In 2013, Target, an American retailer with nearly eighteen hundred stores nationwide, found itself at the center of one of the largest data breaches in history. More than forty million Target customers' debit and credit card information had been exposed. Shoppers left Target in droves in fear that it would happen again. Their confidence had been breached along with their data. The data breach led to CEO Gregg Steinhafel's resignation in 2014 and caused a freefall in Target's store sales. This was a complete failure to recognize an immediate need. Perhaps Steinhafel felt it would go away or that it wasn't that big of a deal. Maybe the PR firm advising Target provided poor advice. No matter, situations like these are examples of immediate needs that must be dealt with in the present, not tomorrow, not next week. A strong public relations campaign may have helped neutralize some degree of customer outrage over the breach. Instead, Steinhafel's approach was to "run for cover" and avoid talking about it. Bad news, unlike fine wine, does not get better with time. Dealing with bad news is an immediate need. If Steinhafel, or the Target board of directors, had recognized this sooner, perhaps they could have done a better job of mitigating their customers' crisis of confidence.

Now that you know where your product or services aligns with a want or need, it's time to talk about how your buyer makes the decision to take action. As critical as it is to understand the difference between a want and a need, it is just as critical to understand your buyer's decision-making process and the journey made on the way to making a purchase.

CHAPTER 4

VISION AND ITS ROLE IN THE BUYER'S JOURNEY

A leader has the vision and conviction that a dream can be achieved. He inspires the power and energy to get it done.
—RALPH NADER

Shared vision, line of sight, and, more recently, the term "alignment" have all been used to shed light on the importance of ensuring all internal stakeholders are on the same page and believe in a shared objective. Teams that attempt to operate with different goals or beliefs rarely succeed, and if they do, it's usually short lived. At some point, reality comes crashing in and ruins the party. The alignment you're looking for should always center around the priorities of the buyers. Their "critical to success" factors—not yours, your team's, or the boss's—are all the reasons for your existence.

There are two principle ingredients to leading an effective buyer's journey. Vision and conviction are the foundational traits that demonstrate strong leadership when working to create a remarkable customer experience.

Vision is a critical characteristic for today's leader. Sure, vision has always been important in leadership roles. Bill Gates, Elon Musk, and, yes, the late Steve Jobs all have possessed this quality. The ability and willingness to see what others can't, or won't, has been their gift of vision. They have seen beyond the curve, around the corner, and miles down the road. Most leaders focus on what's immediately in front of them, which usually manifests itself in the form of an obsession on current-quarter results. Jeff Bezos of Amazon and Sergey Brin and Larry Page of Alphabet (formerly Google) have shyed away from providing guidance to Wall Street on quarterly results. Their reason? Simple. They do not want outsiders to influence their innovative ideas and long-term views to create and build lasting value.

Vision is a quality that we have done our best to squash. As children, we had wild imaginations and believed anything was possible. We were able to take random objects and put them together to make an imaginary spaceship. We constructed entire worlds of make-believe that we played in and explored. Other lands, planets, and places were at the tip of our fingers—right there in the forefront of our minds. As we got older, we learned to not dream so much, to not think too differently from others, and to do our very best to just fit in. Fitting in became our primary goal. Yet history's greatest visionaries pushed back. The great ones never gave up their dreams. They focused, fought, and found people they could excite to support them and their ideas. They found people to follow them.

Tapping back into your ability to envision new ways, or new ideas, requires hard work. To imagine new ways of doing things requires deep and reflective thought. To a large extent it requires a bit of dreaming. For so many years you've worked in the opposite direction, trying to suppress those dreams. Taking time to read, think, and dream are the three primary ingredients to regaining your vision. After all, vision is about creativity, and creativity is about new ideas, new ways of doing things—it's about dreams to a certain degree. Expanding your knowledge allows your mind to stretch and break through the neural pathways that over years have become like ruts in a road. Once your wheel is in the rut, it's hard to get it out, but not impossible with the right tools. Books, webinars, and networking are all tools that can help you get out of that rut, and so is time to simply think and dream.

When conducting buyer-journey work, providing vision is a necessary and helpful element in securing alignment with the team. As you listen to your customers, you will begin to formulate ideas for improvements. Having the skill to create new ways, new methods, or new processes requires imagination and insight. It requires vision.

Conviction is the second trait leaders need in order to gain stakeholder alignment. Conviction, like vision, can be developed and starts with confidence. Confidence comes from having the belief in what it is you say you can do; conviction leads to actually doing it. Our conviction becomes stronger as we gain more experience. Both good and bad experiences help us establish conviction. When you're a child and you feel a hot stove, you develop a strong conviction that instructs you to not touch the hot stove. Likewise, when you have a positive experience, say making an adjustment to your golf swing that results in hitting the ball fifty yards farther, your conviction becomes stronger when standing in the box.

Another example that delineates the difference between confidence and conviction is how I feel about shoveling my driveway in the winter. I have the confidence that I can shovel the snow in the driveway. I'm fit, in shape, and can shovel the entire driveway in about ninety minutes, depending upon how much snow has fallen. However, I do not have the conviction to do it. I'd rather hire it out and spend the time doing something different. Or perhaps I have the confidence to change the oil in my car. But for twenty dollars I can have it done in less than thirty minutes, and I don't have to deal with buying the materials and disposing of the used oil.

In sales, I have great confidence that I can speak to anyone about anything. Conversations thrill me; they excite me; they energize me. I have no problem meeting people and talking with them about their business and their needs. I have, however, experienced times when I lacked the conviction in the product I was selling for any number of reasons. Maybe I was aware of poor service that was being delivered to customers or the fact that sometimes the product I was selling wasn't working as advertised; it wasn't solving the problem it was designed for. In each case where I experienced these disconnects, the companies I worked for expressed the best intentions to fix the problems, but reality being what it is, and human nature having strong tendencies toward denial, those problems simply weren't addressed as they should have been. As such, when I didn't make a sale, I explained it away as a lack of conviction versus a lack of confidence. I simply didn't believe that the product I was selling was right for my buyer's need. When you've lost your conviction in the product you're selling, or the service it delivers, my best advice is to get out and take your talents elsewhere. This may seem like a drastic step for some, but let me assure you, once you develop a reputation as a salesperson willing to do, or say, anything to make a sale, you've begun the slippery process of tarnishing your personal brand. Once your personal brand is tarnished, you will lose the customer's confidence and most likely that of your future buyers.

Establishing your conviction as a leader takes time. It takes insight, data, and intuition. **Conviction equals your confidence, plus data, plus facts.** When those three ingredients are added together, the outcome is your level of conviction. You might be confident, but your data might suggest limited success. You might be confident, but the facts about the marketplace in which you're trying to sell your product tell a different story. The balance of each of these ingredients depends on the leader. It was Apple that introduced Newton, the first PDA (personal digital assistant), in 1993. In less than five years, Newton was scrapped as the market quite definitively rejected it. The data and facts simply said the market wasn't ready. The vision and conviction under John Sculley at Apple were in direct conflict with the data the market presented at that time. Later, Steve Jobs returned to Apple, and after canceling the Newton, he continued the pursuit of developing a handheld device that would change lives and ultimately change the world. His delivery of the iPod in October 2001 marks perhaps one of the greatest introductions of a product in our time, and the product served as the catalyst for so many other technological advancements and innovations. Jobs remained focused and maintained conviction in the importance of handheld computing devices. He was right. Perhaps Newton's failure was simply an example of the market not being ready. Maybe it was the lack of an iTunes store serving as the backbone and infrastructure needed to propel its value. Regardless, Jobs created not just a handheld device but an entire infrastructure to support it, mainly iTunes. His vision and conviction proved his depth of understanding of the buyer's journey.

Buyer-journey work requires great conviction. You will gather an enormous volume of information during this process. You will assess it and create solutions to address the buyer's needs and concerns, and it is at this point in the process that many teams stumble. Even in the face of strong qualitative and quantitative data, executives may get cold feet, lacking the conviction to take action. Acting with conviction requires both a commitment and willingness to take a risk. To a degree, you are placing a bet that the solution you're proposing should be created, built, produced, and delivered to the marketplace.

To gain alignment between the executive and the team mapping the buyer's journey, you will need to combine your findings with your vision and conviction to create a working hypothesis. This should be your guiding charter. When creating your charter, be sure to include the following: what you're testing for, what you believe you will learn, and what the impact will be on the business once you have this learning. It might be a product enhancement, an improvement in the customer process or experience, or a marketing message that better resonates with the buyer. Your hypothesis should offer a best guess on how these changes will affect revenue. How many more customers will be sold, in what time frame, at what dollar amount? Your charter should also include the proposed individual team members you will solicit to serve on the team. Having a strong cross-functional team will help address any fears or concerns surrounding bias. Learning for the sake of learning is nice, but learning for the sake of improvement is far more powerful in business. Having the ability to connect the dots will help you achieve alignment with your internal stakeholders.

CHAPTER 5

THE ART OF THE CUSTOMER INTERVIEW

*Asking the right questions takes as much
skill as giving the right answers.*
—ROBERT HALF

As you prepare to engage your customers and dive into their buying journey, you've got to be prepared. John Wooden, the legendary basketball coach and leadership guru, suggested that once the opportunity presents itself, it's too late to plan. Your team must be prepared for each of your customer interactions. The fact that you're asking your customers to take time out of their day to help you must be recognized. As you prepare for your buyer-journey interviews, follow the steps below:

1. Present a hypothesis of the buyer's journey as you see it.
2. Ask the right questions.
3. Actively listen and document.
4. Engage your customer in brainstorming.
5. Set expectations for next steps.

A Hypothesis of the Buyer's Journey

Gather your cross-functional buyer-journey team and create a buying line. Make the left side of the line the starting point and the right side the end point, or point of purchase. Lead the team in a discussion that identifies all the steps in between. Capture everything. At this stage of your preparation, your goal should be broad; cast a wide net.

As you begin to think about when your buyer recognizes his or her need, write down the activities you believe the buyer does in that phase. Continue to identify all the things the buyer does up to and including making the purchase decision.

It is quite common that your starting buyer-journey map may include dozens of steps. In fact, when doing this work, teams tend to get very granular when thinking through the phases involved in making a purchase. That's OK. In fact, you should encourage more detail. The more steps in the process you can identify, the more effective the team will be in addressing what it believes are the key moments of truth.

A moment of truth refers to the interaction between a customer and a business that gives the customer an opportunity to form an opinion, judgment, or impression of the business. These are powerful emotional points in the buying journey. Moments of truth can make, or break, a buyer's decision. Have your ever run into a store to purchase a pack of gum, a gallon of milk, or a newspaper, and the line for the cashier was so long you left without buying anything? The moment of truth in this example was caused by the length of the cashier line.

E-commerce sites live and die by their moments of truth. Amazon, the retail master of understanding the buyer's journey, has set the bar relative to ease of purchase. The site is always up, always working, and always easy to use. Have you ever gone to a different e-commerce site where you click on a product and get the "hourglass of death"? It keeps spinning and spinning. The site is so slow that perhaps it times out. In that moment of truth, you decide to take your business elsewhere.

Once you've mapped out the buyer's journey as you see it, you now need to create a hypothesis around what you believe it should be. If your journey line is forty steps, perhaps you believe it should be half that. Which steps would you eliminate if you could? What do you think the impact would be to the buyer? Could you monetize it? This hypothesis will become the map you share with your customers to gather their feedback. You're testing your understanding of the process, and your customers are telling you how right, or how far off, you really are.

Asking the right questions

Have you ever tried to boil the ocean? Of course not. While I'm not taking sides on the global warming issue, I would suggest that boiling the ocean would be impossible, barring some catastrophic event like a comet hitting the earth or the Yellowstone volcano erupting. Short of those types of catastrophes, it's both unlikely and unrealistic to attempt to boil the ocean; doing so would result in a serious waste of resources, including time and money. So why do we get caught up in trying to boil the ocean at work? The truth is, we've placed an enormous amount of value on being able to multitask. The problem is that while your brain is certainly one of the most powerful computing tools on the planet, it can only process a couple things at the same time because of the role our emotions play in everything we do. Computers don't get caught up in the emotion of expense reductions, promotions, terminations, or pricing strategy; people do. And what does boiling the ocean have to do with conducting your buyers' interviews? It's simple. You can't ask everything, so focus on some things—the right things.

There are many things you'll want to know, but what is it you really need to know? What are the critical questions you need to ask? Create a list. It's OK to have fifty things you *want* to know as long as you have identified the five things you *need* to know.

Since you have already placed the draft of your buyer-journey map on paper, the one you'll show your customers, begin there. If your hypothesis says that customers check out three providers on average before making their decisions, then formulate some questions around that hypothesis, starting with validating it in the first place.

1. When shopping for a product or service like this, how many providers on average do you consider before making your decision?
2. How did you arrive at that number?
3. What are the criteria you use when including or excluding a provider on that list?
4. Do you weight some more than others?
5. If so, what are the criteria you place greater emphasis on and why?
6. Where do you go to do your research?
7. Is there anyone you typically go to for recommendations or personal endorsements—a trusted advisor?
8. What impact do social media have on your decision-making process? Which sites or apps do you use most frequently and why?
9. Once you've selected a provider and are committed to buying from that provider, how do you establish expectations of what happens next?
10. How do you want to interact with the provider after the sale? If you want a relationship, or if there is one because of the nature of the product or service, what do you want to hear from the provider, when, through what medium, etc.?

Look at each step of your journey map and develop a series of questions for each step: from "how do you become aware of a provider" to "tell me about the set-up process and how you think it could be improved." Also pay special attention to how your buyer wants to be engaged in the future. What's the buyer's idea of creating a relationship? Does the buyer want one? What would it look like? Building lasting relationships with your customers is a necessity, not a luxury. It all begins by asking questions.

Active Listening

Conducting your customer interviews with two to three team members is a great way to capture feedback. Assign one person to be the driver of the interview while the other two are taking notes and watching body language. Companies sometimes hire a professional facilitator to guide

THE CUSTOMER MINDSET

a meeting, and customer-journey work is similar. When leading a discussion, it's difficult to hear everything that's being said, and sometimes even more difficult to pick up on body language.

Active listening requires you to be 100 percent plugged into the discussion. Take notes on what was said and how you perceived the customer's body language. Did the customer back up when a specific question was asked? Did the customer lean forward and change the tone of voice used? Capture the customer's feedback and reactions as specifically as possible. Assign roles to each team member before meeting with the customer. If you're going as a three-person team, make sure everyone knows what his or her role in the interview process. Not everyone can be the Barbara Walters or Bill O'Reilly of the interview. Someone has to be the producer—in the background observing, monitoring, note-taking, and developing follow-up questions based upon the customer's responses.

Part of actively listening is paraphrasing back to the interviewee what you believe you heard. "So your accountant is typically the adviser you look to most for advice? Why?" Or you might say, "You mentioned that you do your payroll every Tuesday morning, but then I understood you to say that you looked for a provider that offered 24-7 service. Tell me, what type of circumstance would require a need for you to speak to a payroll company at four on a Sunday morning?"

When you pay attention to what the buyers are saying, you can enrich the dialogue with them by paraphrasing back what you've heard them say. Many times you'll find buyers having epiphany moments once they hear you recite back their own words. Maybe hearing their words restated, the buyers realize they don't really need to speak to a payroll company at four on a Sunday morning. Maybe the one time they had a problem with payroll happened on a busy Tuesday when they weren't able to get to payroll until seven in the evening and found they needed to speak with someone then. A potential follow-up question using their feedback could be this: "What if there was a provider that offered the service hours of Monday-Friday from seven in the morning to ten at night local time? Would that help?" By using the information your customer provides throughout the interview, you establish credibility, rapport, and, perhaps most importantly, goodwill.

Active Brainstorming
After asking the right questions and then listening for clues or keys as to what motivates the buyer, it's now time to do a little brainstorming with that buyer. Ideation is a great way to engage the buyer in a way that gets him active and involved in improving his own experience while providing you with ideas that can help improve the experiences of other customers at the same time.

The person on your team tasked with taking notes should be collecting and organizing responses throughout the interview. After you've walked through your draft buyer-journey map with the buyer, asked questions, and collected feedback, you've now arrived at the part of the process that allows for an exchange of ideas between you and the buyer. What ifs? How abouts? If we were to do such and such?

Keep in mind that no answer in and of itself should possess so much weight that you change direction, strategy, product features, etc. However, if after you conduct a number of interviews and you find common themes relative to certain ideas, then of course you should dig deeper. Asking the right questions will lead the buyers to providing the valuable insights you need in order to understand their buying journeys. The more time you put into preparing for your journey work, the better the output will be from your buyer interviews. You get what you design.

As you enter into the brainstorming phase with the buyer, be open-minded. Be ready to hear that the buyer would prefer that your product were free, or at least 50 percent less expensive. But would that really change the buying behavior? Why do so many businesses still use ADP or Paychex for their payroll administration rather than using one of dozens of online services available for half the price? Price can't be the only driver. So what is it?

Maybe your customer tells you of a desire for a mobile application to access your service instead of it only being available on a desktop at the office. Why is that? How would it be used? What type of situation would exist in which having a mobile app would improve the buyer's experience or change the buyer's behaviors? If a mobile application would allow the buyer to submit business to you while out in the field, how much more often would the buyer submit business from a smartphone or tablet versus a desktop?

What about online capabilities? In the insurance industry there are fairly predictable changes that occur with an insurance policy during its term. Changes of addresses and phone numbers are some of the common things that insurance brokers need to do on behalf of their insureds. These types of changes do not create any underwriting implications for the insurance carrier, so what if the broker was able to make these changes online versus having to contact the insurance carrier's call center, or, worse yet, its underwriter?

By capturing in detail your customer's responses during the interview, you are better able to circle back to those responses and actively engage the customer in developing ideas to make improvements and innovations.

Setting Next Steps and Expectations

As you get to the end of the buyer interview, it's time to provide a clear set of expectations around what your buyer can expect next. You want the buyer to know that you appreciate the time and input. By providing insight into how you're thinking about next steps, you will further solidify both your appreciation of the buyer's time and ideas surrounding the buyer's journey and how to improve it.

You should already have an idea as to how long it will take to get through all of your buyer interviews. Share this timeline with your buyer, noting whether you're at the beginning stages of these interviews or toward the end. Being able to say, "We've got another four interviews left, which we should have wrapped up by the end of June," will demonstrate your willingness and eagerness to be as open and transparent as you can about the entire process.

How long it will take you to assess all the information you have gathered from the interview process will depend largely upon three factors: the size of your team, the number of buyers you interview, and the experience of the project manager (which I strongly recommend for this work) who is driving the process. If you believe your assessment phase will take three months, then you should inform the buyer that your intentions are to provide an update beginning in early October, assuming you've completed your interviews by the end of June.

The bottom line is to have your buyer feel confident that you intend to take action. You didn't waste his or her time. You believe that there are improvements that can be made and that a clear picture exists relative to how you plan to move forward. If your dates change, a simple e-mail to the buyer about this is imperative. Think of it as a moment of truth. If you say, "I'll be in touch in thirty days," then the expectation has been set, and the buyer will be waiting for an update. If no update is received in that time period, you've missed an important moment of truth, which in turn may cause your buyer to be doubtful of anything you say in the future.

Be as clear as you can as to when you will follow up and what you will be providing in that follow-up discussion. If it changes, be open and let the buyer know why it changed. Honesty and transparency are two of the best characteristics you can offer in all of your communication with your buyers, especially those who gave of their time and ideas to help you in this process.

CHAPTER 6

THE BUYER'S JOURNEY

We all have jobs in our lives that must get done. We reach out and bring products into our lives to get these jobs done. Marketing is all about asking, "What job is the customer trying to accomplish?"
—CLAYTON CHRISTENSEN

Earlier we defined the marketplace as a buyer with a need and a seller with a solution that meets that need. Understanding the marketplace is crucial to your product development and building a competitive and viable business. Finding what motivates each side is crucial to the buyer's journey. Looking solely at what other sellers do to survive and win is a sure way to fail. Too many businesses are hyperfocused on their competition rather than their buyers. Your focus must be on the buyer first and your competition second. Your marketplace, whether you know it or not, is highly competitive and leaves little room for "me-too" companies. These companies offer little differentiation between themselves and others like them. They could be selling a commodity or a very complex or specialized product. Me-too products, and the companies that produce them, provide minimal room for a remarkable customer experience. These companies work feverishly trying to convince the buyer that there is no better way or better solution than what they are offering. They are the antithesis of innovation, and, as such, they tend to ignore their buyer's journey and how it's changing.

Buyers are quick to spot a me-too offering. They assess it, rate it, rank it, and place a value upon it. Most of the time a me-too offer survives solely on price—being the lowest, of course. Since there is little else that provides differentiation of a me-too offer, price becomes the lowest common denominator. If you find yourself, and your company, in the less-than-desired spot of being a me-too provider, this chapter is just for you. Recognizing the steps your buyers go through on their journey to the cash register is critical to developing some level of valued differentiation. Being different for the sake of different adds zero value to the marketplace. But being different in a way that changes the relationship between you, the provider, and your buyer will add great value to your business.

We're all consumers. From air, to food, to energy, to education and beyond, we consume. How we consume continues to evolve in large part due to technology. First, the telephone, then radio, followed by television, computers, mobile phones, tablets, and now watches. Each evolution of technology has altered our behavior as it relates to our consumption of various goods and services. Moore's Law describes a driving force of technology and social change, productivity and economic growth. Gordon E. Moore, the cofounder of Intel, the semiconductor behemoth, observed that the number of transistors incorporated in a chip would double every twenty-four months. Think of an iPhone or microprocessors that went from single core, to dual core, to quad core. The point is that technology continues to drive rapid change in the buyer's journey.

Technology has enabled the flow and availability of information. When information was scarce, the seller was in control. We were forced to believe what we were told and trust in the salesperson's claim regarding product capabilities. Every now and again we would hear about disconnects between what the salesperson said the product did versus what it actually delivered. The Better Business Bureau was the primary—if not only—source of reference checking.

Today, an almost infinite amount of information is available twenty-four hours a day, seven days a week. You can find out almost anything about anybody, any company, product, or service. You can quickly scan reviews on Yelp, Angie's List, Amazon, or Google. It doesn't matter that you don't know any of these people who are providing their reviews. Perhaps an unintended consequence of big data is the availability of buyer reviews across dozens, if not hundreds, of websites. If you find a product or business with five out of five stars, you feel fairly confident in your decision to move forward with your purchase. If you see an average of two out of five stars, your brain says, "They can't all be wrong," and you move on. Twelve, twelve hundred, or twelve thousand strangers provide a review, and today's buyer listens without knowing a single one of them. The buyer simply trusts the data.

For any business to survive and thrive in 2016 and beyond will require it to have an intimate knowledge of the journey its buyer takes on the way to a decision to buy or not buy. Innovative, agile, nimble companies make mapping this journey a priority and an ongoing activity. They recognize that the journey continues to change as it is influenced and adapts to technology—the Moore's Law affect. HubSpot, Forrester and SiriusDecisions have all conducted deep research into the buyer's journey.

While there are some slight disagreements in research from one company to another, what is clear is that buyers today are making more of their decisions on their own via independent education versus the information they receive solely from a sales representative. Whether that number is 20 percent or 70 percent, we know that some portion of the buyer's decision-making process is completed prior to a meeting or interaction with a salesperson—and that percentage continues to grow.

Some stats surrounding this claim include the following:

- "Sixty-seven percent of the buyer's journey is now done digitally."—SiriusDecisions
- "Fifty-seven percent of the purchase decision is complete before a customer even calls a supplier."—CEB

- "Seventy-four percent of business buyers conduct more than half of their research online before making an offline purchase."—Forrester Research

What's clear is that, by and large, most firms agree that a significant portion of the buying process, if not the majority of it, takes place digitally. David Moncur, the founder and CEO of Moncur, a branding and digital agency, says, "Overwhelmingly, customers come to us to help them grow their businesses. The most successful companies understand that the process of growth is driven by effective communication, and have figured out that the medium for that communication is digital. We help them decide what to say, how to say it, as well as where and when it is best communicated, then we help them build and manage those communications—we gain the insights we need to inform the entire process through a deep understanding of the buyer's journey."

Where your buyers shop, and how they shop, should be a key input in developing your go-to-market strategy. Don't assume that your product can only be sold via a salesperson. Or that the only way to advertise is through a brick-and-mortar showroom. Think of Tesla. No dealers. No showrooms—at least not the typical showrooms you think of when shopping for a car. A few strategically placed "stores" across the country are the only visible sign of Tesla. What really sells Tesla? Word of mouth, reputation, and styling. Teslas have a very unique look. They've become more than a status brand. They are an aspirational brand. Owning a Tesla means you've arrived. They've appealed to their buyers' needs by delivering what they want in a vehicle: power, styling, comfort, and, of course, green. They did this by listening and building a vehicle that reflected their buyers' journeys.

Another example of a company that has leveraged its buyers' input is John Deere. By paying attention to its buyers' changing needs, John Deere recognized that soft commodity prices were putting a crimp on farmers' abilities to purchase new equipment. The less a farmer makes, the less he or she has available to purchase a new John Deere. Because of Deere's deep understanding of its buyer's journey, it recognized an unmet need in an area most people wouldn't associate with farming—big data.

Deere's heavy investment in its software demonstrates its belief in and commitment to the idea that by leveraging big data, it can improve its customers' experience, grow their businesses, and ultimately improve their buying journeys. Their machines enable the farmer to gather information, such as the spacing between planted seeds, and transmit that information to a data center. There, the information is analyzed and sent back to the farmer, where he can access it through his mobile device and make changes in real time relating to his planting and harvesting of crops. Who would have thought of John Deere as a software company? The fact that its managers listened and acted on their buyer's needs shows courage, innovation, and leadership. They committed to understanding the journey their buyers traveled in route to making their purchasing decisions.

To begin mapping your buyer's journey, you need seven things:

1. **Clear scope of work**—What do you expect to gain from this work? What's your hypothesis? The only way to determine the effectiveness of your work is to have something to measure it against. You may end up disproving your starting hypothesis after creating your journey map. Remember, the true point of journey mapping isn't about proving what you're doing is right; it's about understanding the customer at a deep enough level in order to provide a better, more remarkable, experience.
2. **Alignment**—One of the most challenging phases of journey mapping takes place before any work begins. Getting alignment is sometimes difficult, but critical, to a successful outcome. Leading this work is typically the responsibility of the marketing team. While most internal scuffles center around who "owns" the customer, I'd propose that the leader of this work should be the one (or team) who has access to customer relationships, buyer insights, data, and the ability to combine it all and assess it. Because of that, marketing should be the driving force in this

work. If your marketing team is responsible for product, price, place, promotion, and (the fifth p) process, then you're placing this invaluable work in the right hands. If marketing for your company is just a place to print brochures, then the answers to these questions will help inform you as to who should be responsible for conducting the buyer-journey work. Assuming it is marketing, this is where, or should be where, your sales data is assessed and evaluated. It's where A/B testing (comparing two versions to each other) happens and where learning is gathered and analyzed. It's where the actual experience delivered is measured against the brand promise through a variety of tools, including everything from the basic customer survey to more robust measurements, such as net promoter score (a measure of a customer's willingness to recommend a company's product or service). Marketing should be driving the creation of buyer personas using this data. Buyer personas provide detailed demographical information that may include gender, title, age, functional area of expertise, memberships, subscriptions, and list of trusted advisers. With these beneficial insights, marketing's lead role is to define the buyer's journey and secure alignment with all stakeholders, especially any executive who could pose an obstacle to this work being conducted.

3. **Cross-functional team**—Since you will be looking at your customer's entire life cycle from start to finish (awareness through purchase, and, hopefully, repurchase) it's important to have a representative from each of the major functional units of the business involved in this process from the beginning. This is *not* just a marketing or sales exercise. Operations, IT, finance, and any other area that provides a customer touch point needs frontline involvement. The team can't be too large, but it needs to have the right team members to be effective. Open-minded and critical thinkers are required. People who are too invested in their way being the right way will only become distractions and obstacles to the team's goal of getting to the truth. In fact, team members should be challengers of the status quo. They should be excited to break things to see just how good they

really worked. They must be curious. They must be inquisitive. They must be customer advocates. Your cross-functional team is the group of people responsible for reengineering the buyer's journey based upon what they've learned, coupled with the resources available.
4. **Diverse and random list of customers**—New customers, existing customers, single users, multiusers. Consider geography. If your product or service is sold nationally, you should have a cross section of customers from different geographies. Why? Because the goal of this process is to determine how your customers buy in order to develop a stronger GTM (go-to-market) strategy. People in the Midwest may have a different buyer persona than those in Silicon Valley or in the Deep South. Having this knowledge will help you build and refine your digital marketing strategy by creating dynamic content and campaigns for these various personas. Your sample size depends on a number of factors, including the following:

   a. Time frame as defined in your scope of work. Are you committing to detailed findings in three months, six months, eighteen months?
   b. The size of your team. While smaller teams tend to be more nimble, they also have capacity constraints. A ten-person team can interview twice as many customers as a five-person team.
   c. Geography. Are all of your customers contained in a specific geography, or are they scattered across the country—or the globe?
   d. Budget. While many companies conduct this work using the telephone, or teleconferencing tools such as FaceTime or Skype, others prefer being eyeball-to-eyeball with their customers. Planes, trains, automobiles, food, etc., all play into determining how large of a sample size you can afford. I strongly suggest that while you may be tempted to use the phone to save money, you should budget for some of these interviews to take place at your customers' locations. Nothing

speaks to commitment more than taking the time to travel to your customer's place of work.

5. **Interview guide.** Consistency is the key to maximizing the results of your buyer-journey work. Having a standard set of questions to ask will help guide each of your customer interactions and provide a level of quality assurance within the process that you're testing and investigating the same areas using a consistent group of questions and directions. In the absence of a standardized interview guide, you risk getting distracted or derailed in your conversation with the buyer. Remember, the goal is to gather enough qualitative and quantitative information to arrive at a conclusion as to how your buyers make their decisions, and in order to reach those conclusions, you need multiple buyers answering the same set of questions to establish themes. While these interviews may differ in length from company to company, and from in-person to phone, you should plan on thirty to sixty minutes of time with each customer. I have participated in interviews as short as twenty minutes and as long as four hours, depending upon the complexity of the product being offered and the degree of engagement in the interview with the customer.

6. **Moments of truth.** While each step in the buyer's journey is important, there are some steps that carry more importance when it comes to delighting or displeasing a customer. These steps are referred to as moments of truth. A moment of truth refers to a specific interaction your customer has during the engagement with your company that places the customer in a position to form an opinion. It could be how you feel when you pull into a Walmart store parking lot. If there are carts everywhere, what does that tell you? Go down the road to Target and the parking lot is clear of carts. One of Target's long-held beliefs is that the customer's first moment of truth is determined by the feeling produced upon arrival at a Target store in terms of the perception of comfort and cleanliness. Another moment of truth may revolve around the opinion you form when you see a clean delivery truck versus a dirty one. Have you ever seen a dirty UPS

truck? In his book about UPS, *Big Brown,* Greg Neimann talks about the importance UPS places on having clean and shiny trucks on the road. It's not uncommon for drivers to have their trucks washed several times a day if they are working in climates with rain or snow that makes the truck dirty. Think about it. Next time you see a UPS truck, check it out. I'll bet it looks as if it just came out of the showroom.

7. **Project manager—a single owner.** Journey mapping is tedious and time consuming. There are several starts and stops throughout the process. It's like building a house. If you've ever built a home, you know that it seems to take forever to get started and break ground. Then one day you drive to your new homesite to find the hole dug for a basement or the slab poured for the foundation. You come back the next day, and the next, and yet nothing has happened. Days or weeks could go by without seeing any activity, and then one day you arrive to find the walls erected and a roof on. Journey mapping is the same. And much like building a home, it requires a foreman to keep things on track. Journey mapping (if done correctly) requires a project manager. Your PM should have strong process and project management skills and possess a personality that is strong enough to corral people when needed and hold folks accountable to their deliverables. An additional trait most helpful for effective project managers is assertiveness. PMs often interact with people who are senior to them in the organization. They must have the intellect, savvy, and assertiveness to drive progress on the projects they are leading. There is a fine line between being assertive and being aggressive. You want your PM to be strong in opinions while being able to listen and consider others. A PM who is a bull in a china shop will turn people off and be ineffective.

Now you're ready to get started. You've got a clear objective, the team is aligned and hopefully excited about the work, and you've got a project leader. Your team has been selected, and executive sponsorship has been secured. This is an exciting time. The journey you're about to embark upon has been developing for some time. You just want to get started. Keeping your optimism and positive outlook will be important. By nature, mapping your buyer's journey and further creating recommendations as to how to improve that journey will present some challenges and frustrations. I want to call attention to three possible obstacles, or caution areas, surrounding journey mapping that may surface at some point during this work:

1. **Internal Skepticism.** You may encounter some folks within your company who will tell you your customers are not interested in spending time with you. They're just too busy and don't have time for this kind of stuff. But I would argue against this misguided belief, given more than a decade of experience doing this work. By and large your customers want to hear from you. In fact, they're desperate to hear from anyone, other than a salesperson, with whom they can share their opinions, experience, and feelings toward your product. So take charge. Be confident in the work you're doing, and push it forward. Remember that what you learn from this process is important, but the goodwill you establish with your buyers will be priceless.
2. **Company Impatience.** The biggest risk area in journey mapping is your company itself. As I've stated earlier, this work is time consuming, and patience, especially within the executive leadership team, can run thin. There may even be a call to end the work before it's completed under the premise that it's taking too long and "we haven't learned anything of value yet." This is why it's so crucial in stage one of the process, when laying out the scope of work, that you communicate a clear time frame for completion. **Provide regular updates to the executives, but resist the urge to showcase early recommendations.** This is a common pitfall for many first-timers doing journey work. One of the fastest ways to get this work shut down is by presenting a half-baked solution. If you presented a twelve-month journey mapping process, provide a monthly update. Your update should include high-level metrics, including the following: number of customers interviewed, categorizations of findings, patterns, themes, etc. But make no recommendations until the work is completed. If there are

changes that lead to an extension of this timeframe, then communicate them as soon as possible. Keeping people in the loop on this work will help keep you from getting stuck in the mud.

3. **Denial.** As I mentioned earlier in the book, I've been blessed to have worked for some great leaders. Vision, courage, discipline, and a deep-rooted passion for excellence drove these leaders to have open minds and a willingness to admit they, and ultimately the company, weren't perfect. That said, I've also experienced leaders who lacked all of these characteristics and began to run for the hills when the feedback wasn't what they wanted to hear. They were in denial. Their reactions ranged for anger to excuses. It costs too much; no one else is offering that level of service; the customer doesn't know. These comments and others like them should be big red flags if they arise. If these are the reactions you're hearing, take note of whether your boss's views are shared across the executive team or if there are others on the team who can serve as your advocates. Perhaps others are thinking a bit more deeply and more clearly and logically about the importance of getting this right. A skittish boss who lacks vision and courage is likely to try to get you stuck in the mud. If this sounds like it could be your circumstance, make sure to give thought to a Plan B. Who will you go to? Who will you ask to support these efforts?

CHAPTER 7

CREATING A BUYER'S PERSONA

The aim of marketing is to know and understand the customer so well the product or service fits him and sells itself.
—*PETER DRUCKER*

Once you've completed your customer interviews, it's likely you'll sit back with your team and wonder how you ever made it this far. Not necessarily how you made it this far on the journey work, but how far your business has come without having these insights.

More often than not, journey teams uncover eye-opening, brain-popping customer insights. After all, that is one of the primary reasons you set out on this expedition—to uncover things you never knew about your buyers. You may learn that the problem your product was designed to solve only works some of the time. You may learn that your customer developed a work-around to deal with a product glitch. You might hear that your customer has logged several complaints and has never heard from anyone in response to those complaints. Remember, an open mind is required for this work. Taking a deep-breathing class before you begin this work might not be a bad idea either. No matter how well you believe you know your business and its customers, this work will reveal something to you that will cause you to pause and skip a breath.

THE CUSTOMER MINDSET

As you gather all this information, you'll begin to see patterns emerge relative to how your buyers make their buying decisions. Nearly every buying journey begins with the buyer becoming aware that a need exists. That moment could come from pain, inconvenience, or by having lunch with a colleague who shares how much faster and cheaper his or her provider is. Regardless of how your buyer has reached the point of starting the buying journey, the next step of awareness is on you. Once that buyer recognizes the need, how will you be found? Where will he or she look?

The first output from your journey work, other than the map itself, should be the creation of a buyer persona. Some companies, depending on the number of products they sell, may have dozens of personas. Even if your business sells one product, if it has a multigeographic distribution, you could still end up with multiple personas. How someone buys toothpaste in Italy is quite different from how a buyer determines the choice of toothpaste in the United States. Selling insurance in the Deep South is different from selling the same policy in Manhattan. While technology may be the deciding factor for a New York City broker, relationship will win the day for a broker in Hilton Head, South Carolina. Knowing those differences and being able to adapt to them demonstrates that you recognize that not every buyer is alike.

There are five steps to building a buyer persona:

1. **Identify the decision-maker.** Are purchases made mostly by males or females? Is it a single buyer making the decision or a committee? Is there an age demographic that has come to light? It doesn't matter whether you've identified a mother who makes the buying decision to use Tide or a committee that makes the decision to go with Paychex over ADP for payroll needs. The point is, you need to understand who's making the ultimate decision. This is the critical first step.
2. **Buying criteria.** Is it price? Is it speed? Is it ease of use? Is it integration with other products or services already in use? Is it

perception? Is it *Made in the USA*? If your product is purchased by one or more executives within a business, it's important to note that the buying criteria of a CEO is different from the criteria of a CFO or CIO. That means your positioning must include all three stakeholders if, in fact, you're presenting to an executive committee to make a decision. If it's a small-business owner who by nature is the CEO, president, CFO, CIO, CMO, etc., you should account for addressing each of these criteria for that one person.

3. **How is your product used?** Whether your product is a personal-care product or a mobile application designed for people on the go, having an understanding of when and how the product is used is important. Scott Cook, the visionary founder of Intuit, created what was called the Follow Me Home method. The purpose of a an FMH was to observe firsthand how the product or service sold was being used in real life. I conducted several FMHs during my tenure with Intuit, watching business owners of all sizes using QuickBooks' payroll solution to pay their employees. I saw numerous distractions that took place each day, from a business owner who brought her baby to work every day to a power outage just as the business owner was about to submit his completed payroll data for the week. Seeing firsthand how your product is used typically results in a few surprises. Many times there's a difference between what people say they do and what they actually do. It's not that they're lying or intending to mislead. It's simply the nature of reality. Imagine having to write down each step to driving a car. How detailed could you make it? Would you remember you need to press your key fob twice to unlock the car, lift up on the handle, place your right foot into the car first, etc.? Sometimes things are just missed for no other reason than the customer just forgot. Sometimes the most obvious things we do each day become such strong habits that we simply forget we're doing them. We're on autopilot.

4. **Identify the media used to gather information.** Where do your buyers go to educate themselves on products and services? A CIO may have a certain publication he defers to when expanding his

thinking and ideas. If he's looking to research a new website platform, he may go to CIO.com or Quora.com to learn about it. At the same time, a CMO working in conjunction with the CIO to develop a new website might take to LinkedIn, Twitter, or, as is quite common, "phone a friend." Some buying decisions are made annually as buyers attend conferences, summits, or trade shows where they can see and use the latest technology and tools to help their businesses execute their strategies. *SiriusDecisions*, a sales and marketing best practices firm, calls this understanding your customers' "watering holes"—where they go to find information and get acquainted with new ideas, concepts, products, etc.

5. **Reasons to believe (RTB).** These are a combination of words and phrases supported by key data points that appeal to a specific persona. Revenue, growth, expansion, and market penetration may resonate with a CEO or CMO. Cost savings, reductions, financing, working capital, leverage, and efficiency ratios may appeal more to a CFO. Cyber security, stability, big data, and SaaS (Software as a Service) solutions would all be key words you would use to attract the attention of a CIO. For a marketing agency communicating with a prospective CMO, it might share an RTB that states that "94 percent of our customers experienced a 400 percent increase in marketing qualified leads, which generated a 5–6 percent increase in revenue." An RTB for a CFO may be that "our accounts payable solution will collect funds owed three times faster than your current process." An RTB is simply a statement of fact that implies a direct benefit to your prospective buyer.

Chapter 8

Disrupting the Market

> *The problem with competition is that it takes away the requirement to set your own path, to invent your own method, to find a new way.*
> —Seth Godin

Let me first say that understanding your competition and the marketplace does not imply that I am suggesting you copy it. Quite the contrary. You're an explorer. Your goal is to find out what's missing. What hasn't yet been found? Where are the gaps? Your goal is to disrupt the market enough to capture the buyer's attention to tell your story. Weaving words together with visual images is the most effective way to communicate. Simple, brief, direct, bold.

Now that you've gone through your buyer's journey and have created detailed personas, it's time to explore the competition. Your purpose in this phase is not to focus on any one thing a competitor is doing or not doing, but to develop an inventory of what exists in the market—who is providing it, at what price, with what level of service, etc.

A good way to approach this phase is to use a traditional SWOT. A SWOT analysis looks at your strengths, weaknesses, opportunities, and threats. Using this tool provides a template to help structure your evaluation of the marketplace. A SWOT is set up in quadrants. See the illustration below.

THE CUSTOMER MINDSET

Photo by annatodica

Conducting a usable and valid SWOT requires insight into the market, trends, and assumptions, and, perhaps most of all, a reliable SWOT analysis depends upon honesty. Many companies struggle with creating a SWOT since it requires them to call attention to the areas that may prevent them from growing, succeeding, or surviving. Countless times I've watched as a SWOT exercise became an exercise in denial. The fact is that all companies, no matter how great they are today, have weaknesses and are faced with threats. A threat might not be from a competitor. A threat may arise from a new government regulation. Think of ObamaCare and all the regulations forced onto the health care system. I'm not taking a position for or against the Affordable Care Act; I am simply providing a valid example of where future threats may come from. Or consider the automobile industry and how government mandates on fuel efficiency affect research and development spending.

As you begin to capture your strengths, weaknesses, opportunities, and threats, you should begin to see a story emerge as to how you shape up against your competition. Your assessment will help provide the insights necessary to address your competition and respond to the differences in your offers.

Elon Musk, the founder and CEO of Tesla, recognized gaps in the electric car market. Styling, power, and range were all missing from the existing electric cars on the market. Most were small and looked so different that they crossed the line into eccentric. Remember the EV1, General Motors' first attempt at an electric car? A turnoff for many people, no matter how green their blood ran. The electric vehicle market also lacked a car that people were confident they could drive for long periods of time without getting stranded by dead batteries. So Musk focused on delivering what the market was lacking by using innovation and reinvention. He found a new way to appeal to car buyers, whether they were green or not. He delivered a luxury-looking automobile that provided power and a long-range driving distance. To speak directly to the buyer's worry about running out of power and getting stranded, each Tesla has a built-in GPS mapping system that shows the driver where the closest charging stations are located, including those that offer express charges—a full charge within an hour.

Another example of a marketplace disruption is Dollar Shave Club. In 2011, Mark Levine and Michael Dubin met at a party and ended up talking about how overpriced razor blades had gotten. Talk about an exciting party. The two conceived a business model that would revolve around providing high-quality razors for about $3 a month for five razors. Now, with more than 1.2 million subscribers and revenue in 2014 of $90 million, the company has been valued at $615 million. Dollar Shave Club's YouTube video title—"Our Blades Are F***ing Great"—has become a beacon for marketers everywhere who have recognized the value in viral. Dubin has built this company by listening and addressing an unmet buyer need. The company continues to innovate and disrupt the market by introducing new products through its edgy advertising while leading a revolution in the razor blade industry, bringing about the rise of new competitors like Harry's, which advertises its German-made blades.

THE CUSTOMER MINDSET

I have one final note on creating disruption in the marketplace.

In 1985, a company called Research in Motion was founded in Waterloo, Ontario, Canada, about an hour's drive west of Toronto. RIM, as it was known, had been working on developing a technology platform in partnership with Ericsson for a two-way paging and wireless e-mail network. Over the next fifteen years, RIM pumped out new technologies focused on handheld devices and networks. In 1999, the company would launch a device that would change the world of connectivity forever. That device was called the BlackBerry.

For more than a decade, RIM was the leader in producing handheld total-communication devices. Technology had taken us from Motorola's big, bricklike mobile phone to the bag phone, the flip phone, and to the ultimate smartphone, combining a phone and computer in a single device. Moore's Law strikes again. For years, companies large and small relied on BlackBerry to provide their teams with that total connectivity, but all that has changed.

A recent market share report shows BlackBerry, the once dominant leader, having less than 1 percent market share of the smartphone market at the end of 2014. Instead, two players that didn't even exist when BlackBerry was first introduced now own the market. Apple's iOS software and Google's Android software are the two dominant platforms for smartphones. Open technology that app developers love makes these two platforms the go-to technologies for individuals and businesses that need to stay connected. This serves as another example of a company that failed to listen to what its buyers needed. The management failed to ask and listen to the buyers, instead choosing to ignore the signs that the marketplace was changing.

In the absence of good market intelligence, you run the risk of racing toward the wrong finish line. If you trip when bowling and throw your ball down the lane next to you and it results in a strike, does it count? Of course not. If you tee off on the sixth hole and your ball ends up on the seventh green, do you putt it in and take the score? Ridiculous. You've got to know where your starting point is relative to your desired end result. Apple looked at what the market was providing via BlackBerry. It researched it, studied it, and, with the great vision of Steve Jobs, envisioned an entirely new solution with the iPhone. BlackBerry's hubris cost it dearly, and in fact may lead to its paying the ultimate price: going out of business.

In the movie *The Godfather Part II*, Al Pacino's character, Michael Corleone, tells one of his underlings to "keep your friends close, but your enemies closer." I'm not suggesting your competitors are your enemies, but it does suggest perhaps a closer attachment than what most companies have today with their competitors. Understanding your competition, their mission, what makes them tick, how their customers feel about them, and how their employees feel about working there are all inputs to consider. From Yelp, to Glassdoor, to Facebook and a hundred other social media sites, keeping an active eye on your competition has never been easier. If you haven't yet done so, now is the time to start watching them.

CHAPTER 9

ESTABLISHING YOUR MARKET POSITION

> *Now it's easy for someone to set up a storefront and reach the entire world in very modest ways. So these technologies that we thought would dis-intermediate traditional sellers gave more people the tools to be sellers. It also changed the balance of power between sellers and buyers.*
> —DANIEL PINK

With all the ground we've covered so far, let's take a minute and take a brief step back. I'd like to pose a question for you to answer now that you have insight into the objective of the buyer's journey and the process for mapping it.

What are your company's goals? What are your objectives? Where do you want to be in terms of market share? If your immediate response is "well, of course, we want to be number one," I'd say your response may be a bit too coy or off the cuff for my taste. I'd even suggest that a reply like that could be a rookie mistake, or at best a slightly misguided reply. Being number one may be exactly what and where your firm wants to be. The question is, are you structured properly to get there?

I once worked for a CEO who set a BHAG (big hairy audacious goal) of reaching $1 billion in sales. His BHAG had no strategy or infrastructure set up to help us achieve the goal. Instead, the CEO believed he could single-handedly get the company their by sheer force. We'd force buyers to buy what we were selling. We'd take on significant debt to acquire companies in our space in order to show growth to potential investors to convince them we were the next big thing. Yet this man never once met with customers, never talked to salespeople or sat with operations, and never listened to customer service calls, of which the majority were complaints. The market position he created was fictional in the sense that he simply was talented enough to get the financials to sing the song he wanted sung but without the foundational pillars to support the business in the long term. He was on a mission to check off the boxes that were most important to him personally, not important to the buyers, employees, or investors. Hubris at its worst.

From the time we were children, we've been taught that being number one is the only place to be. In the comedy *Talladaga Nights* starring Will Ferrell, his character, Ricky Bobby, repeats what his father taught him growing up: "If you're not first, you're last." The fact is, this couldn't be more wrong.

There's a cost to being number one. Do you know what it is? Are you prepared to incur it? It could be advertising, human resources, technology, or profitability. I've always run *from* a company whose sole mission was to be number one. To be the biggest, most unprofitable company isn't a trip I want to sign up for. Of course, I'm not suggesting your positioning statement would say, "Hey, our goal is to be the third-best security company in the country." Imagine that? If you wanted to protect something, and were in need of security services, would you want to hire the third best? Of course not. That's not what you'd say. Instead, your positioning would focus on how great you are at stopping fraud, or how capable and nimble you are in creating a customized security service for your clients. Your stories would be all about how successful you've been at keeping the criminals out and your clients safe. Who cares if you're number one or number ten? You want to know the answer? Only you.

THE CUSTOMER MINDSET

Your position in the market is both defined and determined by your buyers and customers. They hold the ultimate voting right. With either their feet, or their wallets, they decide to buy, not to buy, or return to buy again. Your job is to position your company in a way that resonates with your buyer. How you connect the value your product or service provides to the buyer's need determines the tipping point. The more value you can demonstrate versus the cost of the solution you're providing, the better positioned you will be with your buyer. The illustration below shows how your buyers and customers think about your solution.

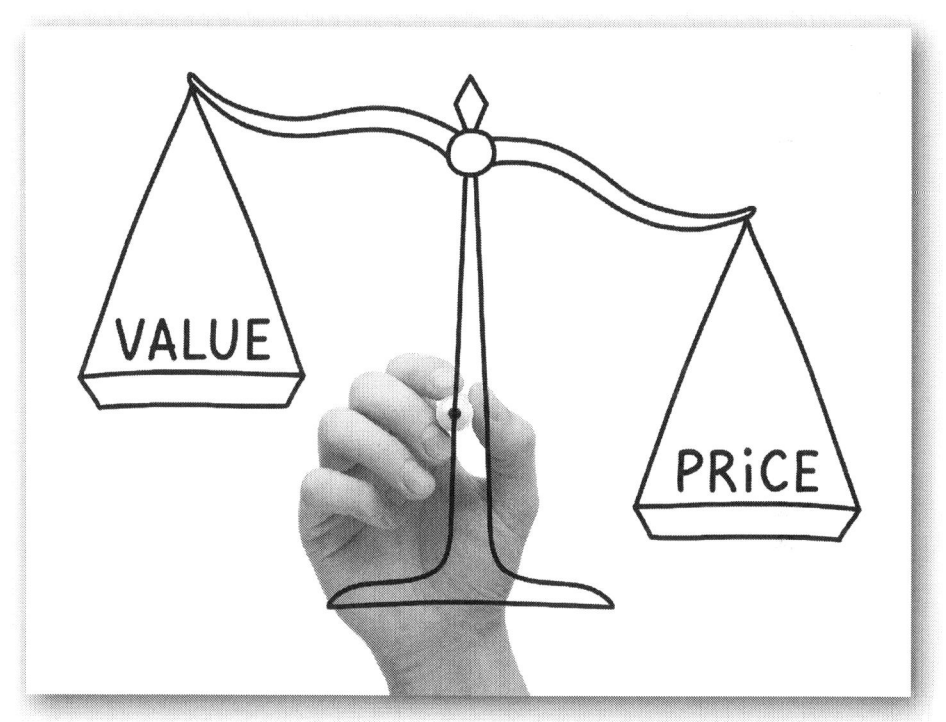

Photo by IvelinRadkov

As you develop your message and positioning statement, be mindful of four things:

1. **Focus on your customer, not you**. People don't care about what you know, or what you can do, until they know you care. Most people believe that if they simply tell enough, or sell enough,

eventually someone will buy. And mathematically they're correct. The problem is, why spend all that time and energy hoping for the customer you'll eventually get instead of focusing on the larger population of buyers, telling them why you care and how you can help them? A typical sales pipeline performs in thirds. One third of what's in the pipeline will always close, one third will never close, and the third in the middle are the prospects that are on the fence. This is the part of the funnel—this middle third—that is in play. It's here that you build your market share. So how do you engage this middle part of the pipeline that's on the fence? An easy and sometimes scary exercise is to do what's called a red/blue test. Take any form of content that your company produces—your website, brochures, sales presentations, or white papers. With a red pen, circle all the following words: "we," "our," "us," and the name of your company throughout the piece of content you're reviewing. With a blue pen, circle the words "you" and "your." If you're like most companies, you'll find you're talking about yourself three times more than you're talking about your customer. That ratio needs to be flipped around. When your message speaks to your buyer, is about your buyer, and demonstrates how you can help your buyer, you're on your way to winning the middle third of the prospect pool.

2. **Showcase customer successes, not your own**. Similar to the point made above, make sure that you're telling your customers and prospective buyers exactly how others who have used your product or service have benefited. In Chapter 3, I talked about RTBs, or reasons to believe. Forget telling your buyers about how long you've been in business. The Great Recession of 2008 erased any value connected to the longevity of a business. Bear Sterns, Lehman Brothers, and AIG, all storied companies and in business for 85–148 years, were brought to their knees. No longer are companies able to tip the value scale using their own history. Likewise, being the number-one provider of a product or service, or saying that 98 percent of your customers love you and stay with you, is also a watered-down marketing message that has become so overused the buyer is numb to it. How do I really know

if you're number one? Do I really care? Or, do I just want to know if you're the best solution for me? The better way to convince the buyer is to instead talk about your current customer successes. Seek out customers who will allow you to use their name in a testimonial. "Main Street America LLC experienced a 22 percent increase in revenue in its first year using ABC Inc.'s solution. Jane Smith, Main Street's CEO said, 'ABC's widget solution helped us improve our sales pipeline velocity, allowing us to sell more clients at a higher average revenue per client.'" Be excited to promote your customers' successes.

3. **Speak your customer's language.** Your work in uncovering your buyer's journey should have identified key words or phrases that resonate with your customers. If your customers talk about growth in terms of adding new clients, then your positioning should include references to new-client growth. If, instead, they refer to growth in revenue terms, your positioning should be about revenue. Recently I had a client whose solution targeted insurance brokers. The client's solution provided brokers with the ability to sell more policies to more customers. The client's positioning, however, referenced how it could help brokers with new business-development efforts. Using these words created an instant disconnect. Brokers think in terms of new written premiums, or book size—not necessarily business development. So I recommended immediately changing the message to reflect the more commonly used broker language. The client now talks about how its solution has helped hundreds of brokers grow their premiums and increase commissions.

4. **Keep it simple; keep it clear.** Buyers have access to too much information. Too many sellers, too many data points, too much noise in the marketplace. Remember, the simpler your message is, the easier it will be for a buyer to connect to you. Your goal is to create a story that is simple and clear. Don't get fooled into thinking that your prospective buyers want or need to know all the details. I've found over the years that the companies with the most complex messages are those that are trying to justify their value. If your value is properly aligned to what you're asking the

buyer to pay, or tilted slightly in the buyer's favor, then your message is a winner. If the scale is tipped in the wrong direction, it's likely you'll lose the prospect to suspicion or doubt. If you're selling speed, show it. If you're selling expense reduction, be clear about it. If you're solving a supply chain problem, show me the process you'll use to improve it. Be simple; be clear.

CHAPTER 10

A FEW WORDS ON PRICING

Price is what you pay. Value is what you get.
—*Warren Buffett*

Throughout my career, I have found there's no topic in business that can cause sparks to fly quicker than a debate about price. What should the price be? Is it too high? Too low? How do you know? I'm not going to get into specific pricing strategies. That would be silly. I don't know your business, your operating expenses, or your commitments to stakeholders. However, I will present a perspective I have on pricing from over twenty years of working intimately with customers in a variety of businesses where I have held executive roles.

Let me start by saying that many things today can be obtained for free. Things that years ago had to be purchased are now free, or much less expensive. The day planner market is almost a distant memory with the advent of the iPhone and Google calendar. Do you remember the last time you saw a Rolodex? No need now that there's LinkedIn and Facebook. Or how about stock trading? Do you pay full price to buy or sell stocks with a traditional broker, or do you use a discount broker—whose fees are not just less, but also who provides the same research and access to the same data that the full-service brokers do?

Today's market focuses on better, faster, cheaper. Notice I didn't say cheapest. The race to the bottom can be quick, painful, and deadly.

Finding the balance between your cost to serve or sell and the price the market is willing to pay is tricky. Publicly traded companies have shareholders to satisfy—making pricing a sensitive topic. In privately held companies, pricing often affects the owner's pocket directly. Having worked for some small, family owned firms, I noticed how having a "lifestyle business" carries over into any pricing discussions. Too often, small-business owners develop tunnel vision relative to price. The more I charge, the more I make. Sounds simple. But simple isn't so simple when it comes to being competitive.

Sometimes being too low priced can hurt a business as well. A friend of mine who owns a large marketing agency bid on a piece of business, which he ultimately won. However, his contact later told him that the board had serious concerns since his price was nearly one-third lower than the next-closest competitor. Being too low made the board pause and question just how good my friend's agency was and whether he would deliver the same, or comparable, quality result of the other higher-priced firms.

Businesses have three choices to make when it comes to setting their price:

1. Price at a premium.
2. Price competitively.
3. Price below competition.

Understanding your buyer and what drives his or her buying behaviors is a necessary factor to consider when establishing your pricing strategy. Even commodities can be priced at a premium. Why do people buy gas from Exxon/Mobil and pay fifty cents to a dollar more per gallon when there's a local gas station next door charging less per gallon? Why do some people by Eggland's Best eggs, which typically cost 30 percent more than store-brand eggs? The answer lies in understanding your buyer, and further, creating a message that resonates with that buyer. Eggland's Best knows it is not going to appeal to everyone. However, the health conscious, organic market is where it will tip the value equation in its favor.

Walmart has built an empire around offering the lowest price in town. Its strategy revolves around selling products at the lowest possible price. When a business chooses a low-price strategy, then all other choices must—must—revolve around that strategy. It's difficult to execute a low-price strategy and operate stores that look like those of Nordstrom. It's challenging to provide the lowest price and hire skilled workers. This is not an indictment of Walmart or any other low-price retailer. It does suggest, however, a simple observation. Do you notice a difference when interacting with a Target customer service representative versus one at Walmart? What's the difference between buying a shirt at Macy's versus Neiman Marcus? Both sell hundred-dollar shirts, but in Neiman Marcus you'll have an apparel expert to help you select the right size, fit, and matching accessories.

If you're priced competitively, but your product or service offers very little that differentiates its value from your competition, it's likely you'll soon run into problems. When products or services that similar are priced equally, the buyer's decision will come down to intangible value—how the buyer *feels* about the purchase. That might be dictated by the reputation of the brand, the friendliness of the salesperson, or the color of the packaging. Options, choices, and configuration are all things the buyer takes into consideration when placing weight on each side of the value scale.

Being clear on your pricing strategy requires communication with your team internally. Apple doesn't discount. An iPhone costs the same at Best Buy as it does from the Apple Store. A Microsoft Surface tablet is the same price at Staples as it is from Amazon.com. These are just two examples of companies that have decided they will not play a pricing game. The price is the price. It's a way to maintain the value of their brand and also create a level of exclusivity. A can of corn, a package of cotton T-shirts, a box of tissues, or a bar of soap are all products that are considered more of a staple item, eliminating the exclusivity discussion. Did you ever meet someone who showed off a Fruit of the Loom T-shirt? Or when was the last time you heard someone touting Green Giant over Birds Eye or a store brand? It simply doesn't happen, or if it does, it's rare. If your price is properly aligned with the value you deliver, the customer will vote with his or her wallet.

There is a mountain of information on the Internet, as well as in books, on the value of A/B testing relative to establishing the right price. Testing for pricing elasticity, the price range across the spectrum the buyer will pay or not pay, is also a very valuable tool to use when establishing your price.

Remember that the more you can differentiate your product or service from your competition, the more likely it is that you'll be able to raise your price. Of course, there is still a ceiling relative to what a buyer is willing to pay, even for a differentiated solution, but the range is wider for testing different pricing levels.

Be sure to include a pricing question in your customer interview. A note of caution. Don't ask your buyer, "Do you think our current price is too high?" You're sure to get a reaction that suggests it is. Instead, ask, "How much would you be willing to pay for this solution if it did A, B, C, and D?" By asking the question this way, you will be able to test for pricing elasticity with your buyers. But be sure to listen to each response carefully. If you conduct twenty buyer interviews, and the buyers all respond by saying they'd be willing to pay 15 percent more if the solution did A through D, then consider 15 percent more. Don't fall into the trap of playing games with buyers by thinking that if they said 15 percent, that means they're really willing to spend 20 percent.

Regardless of how you approach your pricing strategy and what price you ultimately set for your solution, be conscious of this fact: The thing that causes buyers the most pain is the emotional feeling that follows the belief they've been taken advantage of. If you're pricing is not aligned with the value equation, you run the risk of creating this emotional disconnect that can prompt your buyer to go elsewhere.

CHAPTER 11

GETTING THE RIGHT PEOPLE ON THE BUS

Get the right people on the bus, the wrong people off the bus, and the right people in the right seats.
—JIM COLLINS, AUTHOR OF GOOD TO GREAT

In Chapter 3, I talked about the importance of having a cross-functional team in charge of conducting the buyer-journey mapping process. Having representatives from each function of the business that has a customer touch point is critical.

In his book *Good to Great*, Jim Collins talks about having the right people on the bus, and further having the right people in the right seats. Your job is to get the right people on the buyer-journey bus who are excited to be on a journey of curiosity. They must possess the ability and willingness to adjust and flex as the team gathers feedback, new ideas, thoughts, or recommendations the buyer provides throughout the interviewing process. There is a significant body of work surrounding companies that hire attitude as opposed to hiring for position. Of course, having a great attitude doesn't make you a capable programmer or biomedical engineer, but it certainly is the difference maker. John Maxwell, the famous inspirational author who has sold more than nineteen million books worldwide, said, "Your attitude determines your altitude." He's right.

Talking to your buyers and truly listening to them requires a strong level of open-mindedness. People joining the buyer-journey team may have specific backgrounds or areas of expertise, but they need to be adaptable. For example, if every customer you interview complains that your price is too high, the team member representing finance can't become immediately defensive and try to explain why you've priced the product as you have. Remember, customers don't care about your infrastructure needs, your cost to serve, or how much you spend on advertising or the latest technology. Instead, your finance guru should take a superhero approach. What amazing feat can be accomplished by adopting pricing that accommodates the needs of the business while appealing to the customer? Likewise, if the customer complains about the average wait time when calling customer service, this statement cannot be met with an excuse. No one cares how many calls your call center handles each day, week, or month. Customers simply want their calls answered immediately and to have their questions resolved on the first attempt—first-call resolution.

As the leader of this team, your job is to encourage the team to think differently. You're giving team members a license to act, to create, to innovate. Each member of the team is a subject-matter expert. The team members are the ones who, better than anyone else, should have the insight, knowledge, and experience to create new ideas. They are the ones you need to count on to fuel the innovation engine. Your team needs to know two things: the customer's perception is reality, and no idea is a bad one.

If you received feedback from your customer interview that is positive, here's a word of advice: don't get too cozy or comfortable thinking you've nailed it. Buyers can be fickle and can (and do) change their minds at a moment's notice. Likewise, if your feedback is negative, resist the urge to explain it away, or on the flip side, make a knee-jerk decision based solely on that information. No one wants to hear about doing a bad job. But if you can lead your team in a way that allows team members to change their paradigm from "we're not so good," to "now we know how to win," you will inspire your team, build trust and goodwill with your customers, and be on your way to developing a solid business plan backed up by qualitative and quantitative research.

Becoming comfortable with the concept of "there is no bad idea" can prove difficult and challenging even for seasoned buyer-journey teams. Ideation is the process of brainstorming. There are many ways to conduct an ideation session. It could be very casual or extremely formal. It can be done in a team setting or conducted by a professional facilitator. Either way, true innovation comes about by taking the guard rails off of brainstorming and letting your imagination run a bit wild. The goal of ideation is to just imagine. Not an easy thing to do. Most of us find ourselves holding back ideas that we have defined as too crazy, too unrealistic, or too over the top. You may hear someone say that "we've tried that before and it didn't work," or that "there's no way the boss will go for that," or that "we could never do that." Don't allow yourself, or the team, to be drawn into believing there's just one path to success. Push yourself to dream big by answering this question: "If neither money nor technology was a constraint, what would the solution look like—what could we build?"

Placing the right people on the bus will create a team that is comfortable pushing boundaries and challenging the status quo. Some characteristics that make for a great action team include having a sense of humor, an ability to debate, good probing skills, a strong level of curiosity, assertiveness, confidence in the team member's subject matter area, and a desire to win as a team. Traits that should raise a caution flag include any degree of narcissism, a smart wallflower (apprehensive to speak up in group settings), aggressive behavior, or any display that indicates a member already has the answer. George Carlin, the late comedian, had the perfect line for getting out of jury duty. When the potential jurors were being interviewed for the jury, he had a guaranteed approach to getting out of serving. When asked why he'd make a great juror Carlin replied, "Because I can spot a guilty person just—like—that" (with a snap of the fingers). Someone who already knows the answer can create decisiveness within the team. A good working rule for all buyer-journey teams is to leave all egos at the door. Once the team comes together, it's imperative that each team member be able to put on the company hat in place of the functional hat. Being able to conduct this work with a big-picture view is critical. Those unable to leave egos at the door should be kept out. In fact, lock the door. They will do everything in their power to distract and detract.

One final note when building your team is to remember that in most circumstances these folks will not be reporting directly to you. They are "on loan" to you for this journey. As a leader, you need to recognize this immediately and focus your leadership on inspiring action, encouraging thoughtful debate, and driving toward conclusion. Having the right people on the bus will help you do just this.

CHAPTER 12

THE POWER OF "SO WHAT"

*We keep moving forward, opening new doors,
and doing new things, because we're curious and
curiosity keeps leading us down new paths.*
—WALT DISNEY

With the right people on the bus, you can forge ahead with your buyer-journey work. You've got the right people on, and they're in the right seats. You've put open-minded thinkers on the team who have subject-matter expertise but are also excited about the possibility of learning and improving. Assembling this team of broad thinkers will help you get the most out of asking this powerful interview question: "So what?"

As you go through your list of interview questions with your buyer, remember to ask "so what" after gathering the responses to your interview question. If one of your interview questions is meant to lead to an understanding of the required turnaround time for a buyer, then your follow-up should be "so what." Our buyers said his company needs a four-hour turnaround instead of twenty-four hours. So what? Our competition is selling at 20 percent less than our pricing. So what? To make the changes the buyer is asking for would cost the business $1 million. So what? The talent we really need leading this charge would cost us double what we're paying today. So what?

THE CUSTOMER MINDSET

The question "So what?" cuts through all the noise. It's the great neutralizer. If implementing the service level your buyers suggest you need to win their business doubles your cost to serve—so what? Would it mean you could actually charge more for this premium service? Would it force you to look elsewhere for expense savings in order to redirect those resources to where it truly matters—to the customer? Would providing this "white glove" service be a differentiator creating in and of itself a competitive advantage? If so, so what? What would that mean? What would it look like?

If your customer tells you he or she would buy more if your product came in ten different colors—so what? What would it cost you to produce ten different colors? How would it affect production or inventory levels? If you made the change, how much extra would you have to sell? What if having those additional colors allowed you to deepen your existing customer relationships, thereby growing your share of wallet with each existing customer? Perhaps the result of the "so what" question would bring to light a path or idea you might not have thought of previously.

"So what" is like peeling an onion. With every layer, you keep asking "so what" until you get to a stopping point. The customer wants ABC. So what? It will cost us an additional $100,000. So what? We'd have to either raise our price, lower our margins, reduce staff, cut expenses elsewhere, etc. So what, so what, so what, so what? By answering the "so what" question after every layer is peeled back, you are providing your team with more options, more choices, more paths to success. Not every customer request is worth doing. In over ten years of conducting buyer-journey work, I have heard requests that range from the impossible to requests that had already been completed but were never communicated to the customer. Those are always fun.

I was leading buyer-journey work for a company that provided insurance solutions to brokers. In one customer interview, the broker asked for the ability to do simple changes to a policy online. The broker wanted to know why something as common as a change of address couldn't be done online. He couldn't understand why it was necessary to speak to a representative to do this when all the other partners provided this through an online portal. Imagine how embarrassing it was when I told the broker that this level of self-service was actually already available and had been for quite some time. The question "now what" drove us to better understand the importance of communication. Having this functionality available means nothing if it's not being used by the customer. You've done all this work and you're not getting the credit. Worse still, the team is operating with the belief that everyone knows about this. Word to the wise—don't assume your customers know what you do and what you're offering. So what if you don't ask them? You could end up looking like a fool by implying that they missed something. So what? No one wants to look foolish. So what? Well, the "so what" is they have other options, and those options don't include you. Hopefully by this point there's no need to ask another "so what" question.

CHAPTER 13

Putting Things in Motion

> *The secret of getting ahead is getting started.*
> —Mark Twain

Now that you have some ideas on what to fix or improve, it's time to take action. But what first? Sheesh, there's a lot to do. What item or area will you prioritize over all others? As I mentioned in a previous chapter, you simply can't boil the ocean. In fact, **your ability to effect change is only as good as your ability to create the right set of priorities**. In determining your priorities, you must also assess your capabilities as they relate to successfully completing those priorities chosen.

A simple method for getting started on establishing your priorities uses a nine-block table. Along the y-axis is dollar impact to the business, while the x-axis is the complexity to complete. Your categories are low, medium, and high. At this stage of your process, you may not have a lot of detail to assist you in determining how much it will cost or the resources required to complete a priority. Adding a new product feature may require more resources than changing a phone tree. Providing better service training to the team may cost less than developing a new mobile application. Understanding the ratio for time to return on investment is critical to identifying priorities. How long will it take to complete and what is the payback? The point is that you're operating with limited information at this stage, using some data, some experience, and some gut instinct. You're leaning on the team to provide input as to how they view each of these action items within these terms. The illustration below provides a template to use to chart each initiative, its cost to deliver, and the revenue impact to the business.

	Low	Medium	High
$ $ $	Lot of Money Little Impact		Costs a lot to do but yields Big Return
$ $			
$	Forget these items		Low Hanging Fruit

Illustration by Terri DeRosa

THE CUSTOMER MINDSET

Selecting your starting point may also involve your ability to navigate internal stakeholders and politics. Yes, that's right, politics. Your CEO may have a different opinion from the president, who may feel completely different from the head of product development relative to what requires the business's attention first. Bringing your assessment to them along with a strong recommendation is your best bet for securing progress. One of the common pitfalls for buyer-journey teams is allowing this stage to become a democratic process. Sure, you want all to feel as if they have a voice, but remember, no one knows your customer better than you and your team. You've been living it, in the trenches, talking to the customers, seeing what they're doing, how your product interacts with them, and how they interact with it. Your team knows best what the right priorities are, and it's the team's responsibility to propose them.

Plotting priorities in a chart format such as the nine-block grid above provides the appearance, and to some extent the unbiased nature, of your recommendations. You've gone through a process that evaluated the impact to the business from a dollar perspective and the resources needed to complete that specific priority. Using this template reduces the chances you'll be criticized for having a pet project, playing favorites, or, worse, grasping at straws. Also, having your cross-functional team present these findings as their own will neutralize any concerns over favorites.

In addition to the value this template presents, it is also a tool to use to provide updates to the customers who helped you with your buyer-journey mapping. Customers appreciate understanding your business challenges. I'm not suggesting you take them through your monthly cash flow, or lack thereof. But informing them about delivering the product or service you provide, how you do it, the opportunities to improve it, what things stand in your way, and the things you believe could create obstacles brings you closer to your customers.

Many "old school" companies still operate under the premise that they need to shield their customers from operating challenges. The thinking might be that "if we let our customers know where we're falling down, they'll leave us and go to a competitor." Wrong! First, you need to know that your customers already know where you're falling down and what your imperfections are. They know where the gaps are, where your product doesn't work as advertised, or how long it takes to get someone on the line to help with servicing. They know. To think anything different is living in denial. Too many companies, along with some of their executives, already bury their heads in the sand and refuse to believe the truth that's staring them in the face. To them I say, "Hey! Don't be afraid of your customers. Engage them!" To you I say, be brave. Be confident. Show your courage and lead.

Second, you'll find that buyers who feel engaged, and a part of the improvement process, are much more likely to stick with you and give you the benefit of the doubt as you work on creating a remarkable experience for them. Time and time again I've seen customers who go through the buyer-journey process become the strongest advocates for the company, regardless of the obstacles or deficiencies that exist. A consistent comment I've heard from customers over the past decade while doing deep buyer-journey work is a simple "thank-you." Customers by and large don't feel like they have a voice. What's interesting is that social media give the customer more of a voice today than they could have ever imagined having in years past. Each day, customers get more and more comfortable with engaging social media to share their stories, their feelings, and their experiences. Here is my question to you: Will there be someone on the other end to both listen and respond? Or, in contrast, will your customers' comments fall into the black hole and serve as a small ember that ultimately creates the raging inferno?

CHAPTER 14

THE ROLE OF SOCIAL MEDIA IN THE BUYER'S JOURNEY

The power of social media is it forces necessary change.
—ERIK QUALMAN

With hundreds of social media websites today, and new ones sprouting up almost daily, buyers have more choice, more avenues, and more ways to be heard. If used correctly, companies leveraging social media can keep an active check on the pulse of their current buyers' needs and how they may be changing. Social media also offers companies a way to personally connect with their buyers by creating a community that is engaged and conversing. You now know who feels a certain way, who likes what you're doing, and who doesn't. Companies that proactively engage with social media are in a better position than those that don't.

One of the most powerful examples that shows the damage a single customer can create when dissatisfied involved the band Sons of Maxwell and United Airlines.

In 2008, Dave Carroll, the front man for the band Sons of Maxwell, was traveling from Halifax Stanfield Airport to Eppley Field in Omaha, Nebraska. On his layover at Chicago's O'Hare airport, Carroll overheard a passenger talking about having seen baggage handlers throwing guitars around. Upon arrival in Omaha, Carroll found his guitar had, in fact, been damaged. He later learned the cost to fix the damage would run well over $3,000.

Upon his arrival at his destination, Carroll alerted three employees, saying they all "showed complete indifference toward me." He then filed a formal baggage claim, which United declined, stating he didn't file it within the standard twenty-four hour period of time required by the airline. After more than nine months of negotiation with the airline, Carroll finally gave up and decided he would take his anger and frustration out through social media.

Carroll recorded a song and video titled "United Breaks Guitars" and posted it to YouTube on July 6, 2009. Social media was just coming into the public consciousness, and it was still very much in its infancy. However, even at this early stage, Carroll's song attracted fifteen thousand views in the first day. Noticing the popularity of the video, United attempted to contact Carroll and negotiate a dollar amount that would encourage him to take down the video, but the damage was already done. By this point it wasn't about money. The video would stay up.

As of this writing, Dave Carroll's videos on United have been viewed by nearly thirteen million people worldwide. It created a public relations disaster for United that spiraled out of control, most likely due to someone following the rules—not honoring Carroll's claim because it wasn't received within the twenty-four-hour period of time. Within four days of the video posting, United's stock dropped 10 percent, costing shareholders more than $180 million in market value. While it's impossible to say exactly how much this bad press contributed to the drop in market value, you can certainly bet it didn't help things. So was the bad press worth a $3,000 guitar and sticking to the s24-hour claim policy? Probably not.

While United was absorbing the negative body blows from this video, Bob Taylor, owner of Taylor Guitars (Carroll's guitar brand), offered to immediately give Carroll two new Taylor guitars. But Taylor's actions didn't end there. As a result of this incident, Bob Taylor recognized the power of social media for his own brand and launched his very own YouTube site promoting his guitars and full-service repair. One man's junk is another man's treasure. Taylor saw an opportunity arise from the negative publicity that had befallen United, and he seized the moment through social media, and it has become a benefit to his company.

There are countless examples on how buyers are using social media to evaluate your company and decide whether or not they'll do business with you. Remember the Better Business Bureau? The BBB used to be the one to turn to when you wanted to check out a company. The BBB tracked customer complaints—how many were made and how many were still outstanding. Typically you had to wait days to receive the formal report. Now, with sites like Yelp, Trip Advisor, Angie's List, Facebook, Tumblr, and Twitter, you can get immediate access to just about any business anywhere.

Pigalle Restaurant, a Boston eatery, suffered a major public relations nightmare when customer Sandy Tremblay complained about her meal on Facebook. The restaurant replied nine hours later, taking to Facebook with "Hey Sandy, go fuck yourself!" Unfortunately, Pigalle didn't end it there. Somehow, someone felt compelled to go even further, posting a status on Facebook that suggested how "uneducated, unintelligent and unpolished" people were, telling Sandy "fuck you, and don't ever come back." Apparently, management didn't feel that Sandy had a right to complain about a $200 dinner that she didn't like. As of this writing, a Google search shows Pigalle Restaurant in Boston is "permanently closed."

What's your social media strategy?
Earlier you learned about the importance of creating buyer personas. One company that sells one product can have multiple buyer personas. Men and women of all ages and backgrounds buy Crest toothpaste, but each demographic has a different motivation. Some respond to coupons, others to commercials, still others to what their dentist recommends.

There are customers who are price driven for some products where brand is not important, and with other products they will only purchase a specific brand. Your buyer personas will help bring these tendencies to the surface, allowing you to better position your product. Your buyer will take a number of routes to arrive at your door—or that of your competitor. Understanding the importance social media plays with your buyer personas is extremely significant.

Today, Facebook has 1.65 billion users, and more than one billion of those users log on daily. Tumblr has has grown to more than 500 million users with nearly 220 million blogs on their site. Yelp reports more than 142 million unique users to their site every month, and those numbers continue to grow. Buyers everywhere are looking, listening, interacting, and responding to social media every day. They're reading reviews, posting reviews, liking, sharing, tweeting, and blogging to voice their opinions, feelings, and experiences with the people and brands they interact with each day.

Social media has created a global forum for buyers around the world to assist in their buying journey. Whether their purchase involves a new automobile, or something as simple as a quick sandwich for lunch, social media is there to supply the insights buyers crave prior to making a decision. We've transitioned from a society that sought a recommendation from a friend, family member, or trusted advisor, to accepting feedback and advice from complete strangers—and not only being OK with that advice but also acting on it.

As you begin to develop your social media strategy, consider the following questions:

1. Do you have a LinkedIn page for your business? If so, how many followers do you have?
2. Does your business have a Facebook page? How many friends?
3. Twitter? Followers?
4. How often are you posting to these various sites?
5. Do you have established themes for each social site? Do you post different content with different tones to different sites?

6. Are there any comments on Glassdoor from your employees? If so, are they positive, negative, or a mixture?
7. How many reviews have been written on your business via Yelp, Trip Advisor, Angie's List, or any of the other major social sites? What's the tone of those reviews?
8. Are you utilizing photography in your postings?
9. Do you have a blog? How many followers do you have? Are you using links and tags?
10. How many employees of your company contribute to any social media site? Are multiple people posting, or is there one person who does all the posting?

These are a few questions that will help establish a baseline for your social media assessment. It all begins with understanding where your starting point is. Your strategy will differ if you already have a company blog with ten thousand followers versus not having a blog at all. Or if you have five hundred friends on your Facebook page versus ten. And think about the impact Glassdoor has on your company. Your employees are your biggest asset but can quickly become your biggest liability. Treat them well, and you'll deliver remarkable service to your customers. Treat them poorly, and their negative feelings will trickle into your customer experience. Glassdoor is perhaps one of the most underutilized social sites when looking at the buyer's journey. Why? Because most companies still believe that what goes on behind the scenes isn't really all that important. Sure, you'll see a plaque in the lobby touting company values where employees are identified as the company's number-one priority. Yet in practice that's not always the case. Let's explore some typical social media sites and see how they can impact your buyer's journey.

Glassdoor
Dissatisfied workers deliver an unsatisfying customer experience.

How can I make you happy if I'm not happy? If my company's not treating me right, is it possible for me to treat you, my customer, right? Happy employees deliver remarkable service. Their satisfaction on the job just comes through. Have you ever encountered an unhappy employee at Nordstrom? Even on Christmas Eve, the UPS driver who delivered a last-minute package to our door was smiling and said, "Have a Merry Christmas." These companies and others like them know that happy employees are what make the secret sauce for delivering a remarkable experience that consistently delights customers, and a delighted customer means a return customer and perhaps a *raving fan* who will sing your praises loudly enough to attract other new customers.

A 2014 employee satisfaction survey conducted by the Society for Human Resource Management found that 86 percent of employees surveyed said they were "satisfied" with their current job. That sounds like an impressive number. To further validate that number, in 2014, Compensation Force reported the employee turnover rate for all industries in the United States in 2013 was 15.1 percent for that year. It seemed as if all the data aligned, providing the perspective that all was well with employee satisfaction and morale. But was it?

A deep dive into SHRM's satisfaction survey results (which can be found at www.shrm.org), showed some disconnects. While 72 percent of all employees surveyed listed "respectful treatment of all employees at all levels" as their number-one issue, only 33 percent of employees surveyed were satisfied in this area. That's a major red flag! Seven out of ten employees felt very strongly about a specific issue, yet only three in ten felt that issue was satisfactory. Another troubling category was the second-most-important item to employees: trust between employees and the senior management team. Here, 64 percent of employees indicated this was the number-two-most-important item, and only 28 percent of employees felt "satisfied" within this category.

What this shows is that I can be satisfied in the work I'm doing, the job I'm performing, and the stuff I produce every day, all while being completely dissatisfied with the leadership of the company, the lack of vision, lack of trust, or how I feel about my compensation. Think about it. Has anyone ever asked you this question: If money were no object, what would you want to do—what job would you want? The fact is, if we were able to make decisions to do what really inspired us and created passion for us, many of us would be doing something different than what we are currently doing. This takes strength and courage. While we've shifted our economy from one of industrial manufacturing to service, we are still operating to a large extent on a hamster wheel. We go into the office every day, do what we do, and leave at five in the evening. Our workplaces are sterile, numbing to the senses. Some may argue they're designed that way intentionally to keep people in. Give them enough to keep them going but no more.

As your buyers begin to dig a bit on your company during their awareness phase of their journey, uncovering negative information about your company at this early stage is sure to give them pause about giving their business to you. If a company has a low score on Glassdoor, it sends a negative message into the marketplace. The question that is raised is simple: if you don't treat your employees well, how can I trust you to treat me, your customer, any better?

LinkedIn
Now, "whom you know" is available for everyone to see. If I'm interested in you or your firm, I'm going to look to see where we have common connections and then check you out.

Most companies agree that LinkedIn is the dominant social channel for businesses. However, this is not true across the board. Having a LinkedIn profile is an absolute must for businesspeople. But what about having a profile for your business? Is LinkedIn the right social medium for any size business? The answer is, it depends.

There are three critical questions to answer with respect to whether or not having a LinkedIn page for your business provides any value:

1. How big is your business?
2. How active will you be on LinkedIn?
3. How many customers do you currently have?

The size of your business does matter when prioritizing which social media channels you should use. Companies of a certain size and industry should automatically have a LinkedIn page and profile. Here's a guideline for determining if your company should have a LinkedIn page:

- If you are in the B2B or B2B2C space.
- You have more than twenty-five employees.
- Current revenue is in excess of $5 million.
- Your product or service has a mobile application.
- You have a company blog.
- At least one person in your company is responsible for managing social media.
- More than 10 percent of your business comes from current customer referrals.

If you answered yes to all, or most, of the questions above, you should consider creating a company LinkedIn page. This means that people are looking for you or looking for a product or service like yours. LinkedIn will be yet another destination on their buying journey during their vetting process.

Facebook
There's a certain truth to the pressure of "keeping up with the Joneses."

There are 1.65 billion Facebook users globally. More than half of these users are female. Women, on average, use social media for personal use more than men. Conversely, men use social media for business more than women. Nearly 50 percent of users between eighteen and thirty-four years old check Facebook immediately upon waking up in the morning. Of this group, 28 percent check Facebook before getting out of bed. These are critical data points for businesses considering using Facebook as a part of their social media strategy.

One of the most popular comments from CEOs of companies under $100 million in revenue relative to using Facebook as a part of their social media sales strategy is this: "People aren't shopping for our products and services on Facebook. We'll never get a customer from Facebook." Perhaps. Perhaps you never will get a new customer from having a Facebook presence. But think about this:

Facebook has become the go-to medium for people to "air it out" with their friends. The good, the bad, the ugly. Roughly five billion pieces of content are shared daily on Facebook. That means that not only are you hearing about the experience your friend had with a certain brand, but you're able to hear about your friend's friends experience as well—and their friends, and theirs, etc. We've all read posts from friends who complain about bad meals, horrible contractors, a haircut that went south, or the rudeness of a customer service rep.

So while you may never generate a new customer from having a Facebook page, you most certainly might be able to save one. Instead of taking Pigalle's approach of becoming belligerent with the customer who complained about her meal, imagine if the owner or chef replied back with an apology and a free meal and bottle of wine the next time Sandy Tremblay dined with them. Imagine the power of that type of response. Maybe they'd still be in business.

Other marketing data points surrounding Facebook usage indicate that Thursdays and Fridays are the best days of the week for user engagement. In fact, better by 18 percent over all other days. Additionally, the highest usage comes between the hours of one and three in the afternoon local time. Understanding how this social platform is used is an important part of understanding if, and how, you incorporate Facebook into your social media selling strategy.

Twitter
As much as you can communicate in 140 characters or less!

Twitter is one of the more challenging social platforms for most businesses to understand. It's also the channel that demands the highest degree of engagement from a company standpoint. To be effective requires just one thing: regular tweets. And herein lies the challenge.

Best practices suggest that to be effective in building a base of Twitter followers, you must do these things:

1. Tweet six to eight times daily
2. Proper use of hashtags
3. Including people and companies in your tweets using "@"
4. Brief, bold messaging using key words
5. Tweeting value-added content, content that pertains to the base of followers you're trying to attract and develop
6. Use of a scheduling tool such as HubSpot or Hootsuite so you can write your tweets in advance and schedule them to post into the future

Committing to, and staying disciplined to, this volume of content creation can seem daunting. Basically you need to pump out six to eight thoughts a day. Whoa! That's a lot of content. What if I don't have six original thoughts each day? The answer is simple—share other tweets. Part of effective tweeting is to follow the right tweeters. If your business offers a B2B service for small businesses, you should connect and follow tweeters who specialize in small business. If your business sells accounting services to individuals, you should look for organizations that tweet about IRS changes, tax advantages and consequences, or government regulations. By following the right tweeters, you can reach at least half of your daily tweet volume by simply sharing other tweeters' content. Completely fine, completely acceptable, and that still gives you the credit of tweeting.

A final thought on social media

Having a budget to manage social media is not a luxury. It's a requirement for businesses of every size. Of course, it's a bigger issue for smaller businesses to manage than large firms like United Airlines, General Motors, or Nike. But as we've seen from previous examples, even the behemoths struggle and fall down with managing social media. The small-business owner simply needs to be plugged in. When consulting with small- business owners, I always recommend that the owner should have direct access to the company's Facebook page so he or she can see the activity firsthand and reply to posts. Is it one more thing to do? Yes, it is. But if there's no one there to listen and respond to the customer's complaint, question, or concern, it's in effect leaving a vacuum for someone else to fill, and chances are it won't be filled with pleasantries and positives. Are you willing to take that risk?

CHAPTER 15

DEVELOPING YOUR CONTENT STRATEGY

> *By creating fantastic content and spending zero time on audience development, you are certain that you will not succeed on YouTube. You have to focus on audience development as much as you focus on creating content.*
> —ROBERT KYNCI

While content may be king, having the right context is the queen. Knowing what's important—what's useful, valuable, and interesting—is one of the biggest decisions you need to make coming out of your buyer-journey work. Content for the sake of content isn't always positive. More content isn't always a good thing. If the content you're producing isn't hitting the right note—addressing the buyer's biggest concerns or questions—then it has fallen on deaf ears. To make things worse, you may not have only wasted resources to produce this content, but you may have also hurt your brand image by producing content that lacks value. Any negative association with your brand will ultimately cost you far more than the cost of the campaign that generated the negative view. So how do you know what type of content your customers value? Ask them.

Allow your customers to direct your content strategy. Assuming you dove into this area during your journey work, it's now time to act on it. **If** you didn't, stop reading here and go back and create a list of questions on the types of content your customers look for, where they look for it, and the ideal length they're willing to read.

Square 2 Marketing, an inbound marketing agency in Philadelphia, works with companies of varying sizes to create "free reports" to use to generate inbound demand. In an interview with Eric Keiles, the founder and chief marketing officer of Square 2 Marketing, he said, "Customers and prospects alike have so limited time today. At the beginning of the buying process, most buyers are simply looking for information to help them on their buying journey. Simple information that is easy to consume is very effective (e.g., Six building blocks of an effective…, Nine mistakes to avoid…, etc.) This type of content quickly acknowledges their needs and provides a high-level look into the solution that meets that need. We believe that content that is no longer than two to three pages is the perfect length to convert the buyer from visitor to lead and then on to the next step of the buying journey. Long-form content (e.g., white papers) is useful in more complex sales processes, and it is typically twenty or more pages in length and often is a deterrent to the buyer at the top of the funnel. That content is much more effective in the middle of the funnel. Buyers are much more likely to read and absorb a couple of pages versus a couple of dozen pages, so short-form content is used at the top and long-form in the middle."

With a near-infinite amount of information available in digital form, your challenge will be to produce content that is crisp, clear, and concise. Not every piece of content needs to be highly detailed and granular. Often your buyer simply wants to know there's a better way. If you can convince that buyer in a couple of pages that you have the answer, then the buyer will take the time to investigate further.

Most CMOs will agree that consumable content needs to be written at a grade-school level. Whether that's fourth, fifth, or sixth grade is debatable. What we know is that most people "can" read around an eighth- or ninth-grade level, but when they do, they hate it; they much prefer reading at a fifth-grade level. Rather than focusing on writing content for a fifth-grader, I would suggest this—just write simply.

Authors, bloggers, teachers, and many executives become enamored with their arsenal of ten-dollar vocabulary words. They believe the bigger the words, the more points they'll score with the customer. Hey, this isn't Scrabble! It's a game of simplicity. The fact is that **people buy if it's simple; they run from the complex**. We've evolved into a society that thirsts for simplicity. Quick food, fast tax returns, rapid oil changes, and lightning- fast Internet service are the things that we gravitate toward. We seek them out. Who would go somewhere for an hour oil change when there are a number of places that get it done in twenty minutes? Who wants to go back to dial-up service when every day there seems to be an even faster network than what existed yesterday? People want fast, and to be fast you have to be simple.

During my time at Intuit, Scott Cook coined the phrase "drop-dead simple." No matter what business unit you were in, what product you were managing, or what new service you were trying to invent, the key to success was making it drop-dead simple. Just like Disney World's "backstage" strategy of keeping certain things away from the guests' view, Cook impressed on the entire company the need to keep the complex backstage. No matter how difficult it was to create, whatever the customer saw and did had to be simple. All the rest would be hidden, not in a deceitful way, but with the idea that the customer's viewpoint is in line with the old saying, "I don't need to know how the sausage is made."

Creating simple content isn't about treating your buyers like they are a bunch of eleven- year-olds. It's not about making them feel less than capable of understanding how complex things really are. No. Creating simple content is about one thing, and one thing only: respecting your buyer's time. Here's a typical buying scenario:

A prospective customer sits down with two different salespeople. The first goes through a two-hour presentation talking all about the salesperson's company, how long it's been in business, and how complex its systems are in order to handle the buyer's needs. The message the customer is hearing is "you need someone who has really complex stuff, that can address your complex stuff, and hopefully at the end of the day all the complex stuff will be dealt with properly."

The second salesperson meets with this prospect for one hour. During that time, the salesperson acknowledges the complexity of the prospect's needs, but instead of getting a complex explanation, the customer is told how "simple" the systems are that allow the customers to do all this work in a quick and easy way. The prospect is assured that the reason the salesperson's company is so good and trusted by so many is because it makes things so easy.

Which salesperson do you think wins the deal? If the price is the same, the second salesperson wins hands down. If the price of the second salesperson's solution is more, that salesperson is still likely to win the day given his or her ability to remove the complexity and show a perceived time savings. Bottom line is that every customer wants simple, fast, and reliable solutions. And for that, many are more than willing to pay a premium.

Considerations for creating your content:

1. Intent of content
2. The buyer's persona
3. Medium dictates content
4. Marketing automation
5. A/B testing

Intent of Content

In his book *Alice in Wonderland*, Lewis Carroll writes, "If you don't know where you are going, any road will get you there." Not having an ending point, or a goal, makes accomplishing anything rather difficult. Setting clear goals is the best way to ensure you'll achieve them. Perhaps you reach the goal, perhaps you don't. No matter. If you have something to set your sights on, at the very least you'll have results you can measure to understand what you did right or where you went wrong.

There are four main buyer emotions within the typical awareness-through-consideration stages of the buyer's journey. The include **awareness, familiarity, confidence, and conviction**. Within each of these stages, the buyer is focused on satisfying that specific phase before moving on to the next phase. For each of these four phases, the role that content plays is different. Awareness might be a sound bite, a picture of your logo, an e-mail, postcard, or your website. However, during the confidence-building phase, content should include reasons to believe, testimonials, demos, or other proof points that demonstrate your ability to solve the buyer's problem and meet his or her needs. Let's explore in a bit more detail the intent of content as it relates to each of these emotional buying phases and some ideas for how to best create it.

1. **Awareness.** Building awareness is the first step to having an opportunity to engage the buyer. If the buyer doesn't know of you, then it's unlikely you will be considered in the decision-making process. At the early stage of awareness, it's about capturing attention, creating intrigue, gaining the buyer's interest. Establishing awareness is creating a simple understanding of what you do and what problem you solve. It could be a quick message that says, "More than ten thousand business owners can't be wrong." Or it could start, "Taking the pain out of…" Or it could say, "We're growing! We are hiring ten new sales people." These quick, simple, hard-hitting messages are important to building your brand's awareness. They should be short and simple, with high frequency. When building awareness, there is a high degree of value on shelf space. Being where your buyers can see you and find you is essential. Tweeting one time that you're growing won't build awareness. But if you tweet five times that you're growing, post your hiring message on LinkedIn (tied to Twitter via a solution like Hootsuite), and place a banner on your website that validates this message when visitors arrive there, you have a great chance of building awareness of who you are and what you do.

THE CUSTOMER MINDSET

2. **Familiarity.** Moving beyond awareness, your goal is to get your buyer familiar with you. What exactly does that mean? Familiar? I may be "aware" of the guy who runs beside me every morning at the gym on the treadmill, but I might not be familiar with the fact that he's a policeman or an accountant. Being familiar with something says we have a deeper level of understanding surrounding a specific person, thing, product, or business. Now that your buyer knows your name, it's time to provide more detail. The buyer may know you sell payroll software, but does that knowledge extend to awareness that you have the best mobile payroll application on the market? That's familiarity. During this stage, the purpose of content is to go a bit deeper. Creating free reports, product briefs, case studies, and testimonials are all effective ways to increase your brand's familiarity. Be conscious of the length and copy itself. Remember, you're only one step above awareness at this point, so brevity is still important. You most likely have not earned the buyer's permission to provide highly detailed or technical information at this stage. So, like painting a portrait, you paint the base layer first—your awareness stage—and then paint the second layer, which provides more definition, thereby bringing what you are painting into view—your familiarity.

3. **Confidence.** Is it possible for content to establish confidence? I would submit it is. That said, building your buyer's confidence doesn't happen in a single piece of content, no matter how well-developed and produced it is. But if done in a way where one piece of content builds upon another, it is entirely plausible that content can create confidence. Confidence creators typically show up in the form of case studies and testimonials. This type of content demonstrates to the buyer how your solution was applied to a problem similar to that of the buyer and how it worked. Remember, today's buyer is completely comfortable not knowing the reviewer or provider of the testimonial. Due to social media, buyers have become accustomed to and comfortable with third-party reviews. During the confidence stage, you may also want to incorporate a sales contact in conjunction with a specific piece of

content. Whether you use a field or inside sales team, deploying one of those sales resources to assist in developing the buyer's confidence is a key step toward moving that buyer to the conviction stage.
4. **Conviction.** The last and final phase of emotions the buyer goes through to reach the buying decision is the conviction phase. At conviction, the buyer believes he or she has all the information necessary to confidently purchase the solution that solves the problem. This is the culmination of the previous three phases, and it's the most important phase. It propels buyers into action—the action to buy. Content for this phase is not about selling or telling. Content at this phase serves two purposes: to reassure the buyer that the right choice has been made, and to thank the buyer for allowing you to be of service.

The Buyer's Persona

The detailed buyer's personas you've already created should provide insight into topics, types, and mix of content. Your personas have also provided insight into your buyer's watering holes—where that buyer finds research and information. If your buyer is highly technical, then your content will likely need to provide technical insight. If your buyer is a senior financial executive, then your content should offer specific themes and tones that address the buyer's financial questions.

Whether you produce a two-page brief or a thirty-page white paper all depends on the buyer you're trying to communicate with and understanding which emotional buying phase is in progress.

Understanding your audience and where it is in the buying process is critical to developing engaging and actionable content. Is your buyer male or female? Is the need you're solving a business or consumer need? Is it B2B, B2C, or B2B2C? Does your buyer spend time conducting deep research on the Internet, in a store, with friends, via social media, or through specific print media? If your product's target audience is female, employed, making more than $70,000 a year, and owns her home, you may want to consider advertising in *People* magazine, whose demographics serve as a perfect match to this audience. However, if your product is geared toward a seventy-year-old male, you may want to consider placing your message on The Weather Channel or in the local newspaper since 95 percent and 84 percent, respectively, of men over sixty years of age use these media regularly. If your primary buyer is a female midlevel manager of a small company with less than $100 million in annual revenue and whose business is providing payroll services to small companies, you may want to consider placing your message with the Independent Payroll Providers Association or the Women's Small Business Association's website. The point is, you need to understand your buyer and where that buyer goes to conduct research.

Your buyer's personas will provide insights into the content that would generate the highest level of engagement. Once you understand your various personas, you can begin content development leveraging the specifics you've uncovered from each persona.

Medium Informs Content

Developing content for Twitter is very different from developing content for a blog. First, let's look at the obvious. Twitter limits you to 140 characters. Say all you want, as long as it doesn't exceed 140 characters. And remember that's 140 characters, not words—and spaces count too! If your message is going to be placed in a blog, it should be somewhere between three hundred and six hundred words, headlined with a picture that is associated with the topic, and containing links, tags, and key words.

When communicating on social networks, your tone can be casual, fun, personal, conversational. The content you develop should align with the medium through which you are communicating. Use casual content for social media and more formal content for white papers, websites, and product briefs. Approach the content you create for Facebook as if you were writing a friend, or at the very least someone you may know a bit better than an acquaintance. However, when you're creating content for your website or other forms of digital marketing media, your content should reflect a bit more of a formal tone. Not stuffy, but not as casual as what you might be using for Facebook, Twitter, Instagram, etc.

Leveraging multiple channels through which you communicate your message is a great way to demonstrate the depth and breadth of your company. Being able to effectively navigate between a casual medium and something more formal sends a message to the buyer that you recognize there's a time and a place for everything.

Most sales professionals know they need to have a thirty-second elevator pitch ready for quick and informal interactions. The purpose of this pitch serves as a sound bite to set the hook, to garner attention, to generate interest. Most elevator pitches are quite informal, and that's exactly how they're designed. But when that same salesperson is invited in to make a presentation to a business owner, executive, etc., there is a different expectation. If the salesperson shows up and attempts to be as informal as his first encounter was with the buyer, he'll likely lose. Instead the salesperson should take a different approach, a more formal approach. He recognizes, acknowledges, and respects the buyer's time by being punctual, buttoned up, prepared, and professional. He knows his medium has changed, and he changes with it. Ignoring this change results in failure.

Many companies have employees who are solely focused on maintaining and managing the company's social media interactions. These folks are highly skilled in this real-time, fast, responsive medium. They know that social media is a dialogue and, as such, it requires their responses to be friendly and engaging, if not immediate. Their goal is to establish a dialogue with the buyer in order to build credibility and rapport. Social media representatives are experts in engagement. They are skilled in the art of making virtual friends by being creative with their words, tone, and message. However, your social media representative may not be the best-suited associate to create a white paper, exhibit at an upcoming trade show, or respond to an inquiry via your investor relations site. Understanding and recognizing your talent and where it is best used is as important as recognizing the various channels through which you will distribute your message.

Marketing Automation

Gone are the days when marketing was pure overhead to a business's operations. It was the department you called to order brochures, coordinate a trade show, and order those nifty tchotchkes (trinket) that were in such demand. Marketing fought for it's existence during business downturns, and it expanded with big budgets when times were good. The head of marketing was on a constant presentation treadmill, working to justify personal and team efforts. It was pure art anchored by some educated guesses, a lot of gut feel, and many times some gambles, shots in the dark, and coin tosses. The fact is that until recently, marketing's ROI was tough to pin down. That is, until marketing automation arrived.

In the past decade, new tools have hit the market, providing marketers, their teams, and their bosses with the ability to see in detail what outcomes were being driven by the work the marketing team performed. Over the past few years, these tools have continued to improve and are largely considered a must for marketing organizations of any size. In fact, size has no bearing on whether or not a marketing automation system is justified. One could argue that the smaller the company, the more important it is to have a tool such as this available to help generate revenue.

There are dozens of marketing automation systems available today. Most are SaaS-based solutions, meaning you're "renting" or paying a regular and recurring licensing or subscription fee for the use of the service. The service is centrally hosted by the provider, which allows the purchasing company to access a robust tool without having to incur the IT expense of learning, maintaining, and administering the system.

How do you determine which marketing automation tool is best for you? Your decision may be based on a number of factors. In fact, I would hope it's based on a number of factors and not price alone. That said, I also recognize that sometimes just the act of getting started with taking action is better than waiting for perfect. The good news is that there's a solution to fit just about any budget.

First, let's look at the difference between a sales customer relationship management system and a marketing automation platform—this is one of the most common points of confusion for sales and marketing leaders alike. A sales CRM—as offered through Salesforce.com, Goldmine, or Act—is primarily used to manage your interactions with your current customers and prospects. Behaving similar to a giant Rolodex—including your contact names, addresses, and key tasks occurring in the past, present, and future—a CRM helps manage your salespeople's outbound activities. A marketing automation tool operates quite differently. While solutions through HubSpot, Marketo, and Silverpop all contain customer and prospect data, that's about where the similarities end relative to CRMs. A marketing automation tool is used to measure the customer's, or prospect's, engagement and activities level with your company. These tools enable you to measure top-of-the-funnel workflows that show when a buyer visited your website, opened an e-mail, downloaded a specific piece of content, and filled out a form. Using marketing automation enables you to align your future messaging—often referred to as dynamic content—to your buyer's journey. As your buyer moves along the buying spectrum, changing the engagement, the desire for content, and the frequency of consumption of information, your marketing automation platform can react, anticipating the buyer's next move.

Typical features that are included with many of today's marketing automation platforms include landing pages, social media marketing, mobile marketing, e-mail marketing, campaign and lead management, content and SEO tools, and analytics. The complexity of your needs may narrow down the field of marketing automation providers. At the low end of the price range is HubSpot. This offers an incredibly powerful tool, so don't let the price point fool you. Having used this SaaS platform, I can vouch for just how robust and easy to use it is. Campaigns, social media, and analytics functions are very strong with HubSpot. Of course, on the other end of the spectrum is Oracle's Eloqua platform.

This solution, while it is also a very robust platform, is much better suited to a larger enterprise, based on my experience. In fact, most content within the public domain would show HubSpot and Act-On as solutions for businesses with fewer than fifty employees. With more than fifty but below five hundred employees, a company might turn to Marketo, Pardot, and Silverpop as the go-to solutions. Above the five hundred–employee space is considered the area for "enterprise" solutions, where Eloqua (Oracle), Sitecore, Adobe, Infor, and Teradata sit. The best approach is to determine your engagement strategy based upon your buyer-journey findings, select two to three providers for your business size, and ask for a demo. While just about all of these platforms allow for e-mail marketing and social media marketing, the ease of use from platform to platform may differ. You want to select the tool that's the best fit for what you need and the best fit for your own technical competencies, revolving around ease of use.

A/B Testing

A/B testing is all about discovery and validation of your marketing strategy; it's hypothesis based. We believe if we promote this product, at this price, in this color, we will sell X number of widgets. Or we believe that placing a circular button on our home page saying "Act Now" will drive more leads than a button that says, "Click Here for More Information." The point is that A/B testing is just that; you're testing to see which does better, offer A or offer B.

As you go through your buyer's journey, you will have most certainly uncovered some common themes. You may even feel confident making a declaration that all buyers buy this way or that way. I'd urge you to resist that type of thinking. No two buyers act the same in every circumstance. Price, size, shape, color, features, recommendations, reviews, and a number of other factors play into their buying decision. Remember, you're an explorer. A scientist of the marketing sort. It's your job to constantly be asking "so what?" If I change the location of the button on the home page, so what? If I change the color, the shape, the font, so what?

Whether the marketing automation platform you selected provides A/B testing or not, you need to conduct this work. Of course it's much easier to do using a platform that has this capability built into it, but if not, doing A/B testing manually isn't the end of the world. Remember the old Pepsi blind taste-test commercials in the early 1990s? That's A/B testing. Or the Tide laundry detergent coupon that comes in the Sunday paper? Last week the coupon was for two dollars off the purchase of two Tide bottles; this week the coupon is for one dollar off of one. Which works better?

At the heart of A/B testing is curiosity. What will buyers respond to? Which offer will deliver the best results? Which offer delivers the best conversion rates across the lead- management spectrum? These are key questions that every marketer should be asking along each stage of your buyer's journey, and A/B testing is a proven method for answering them.

CHAPTER 16

A Final Word on the Buyer's Journey

Taking the first step to better understanding your buyer is exciting. So much to learn, so much to uncover, so many areas to discover. Following the approach I've laid out in the previous chapters will provide you with a reliable framework to begin your exploration of your buyer's journey. Here are some final thoughts for making the most of this important work:

- Be open-minded.
- Be willing to learn.
- Be willing to say you got it wrong.
- Try new things.
- Believe what your buyer is telling you.
- Be willing to take a hit—not everyone on your team is going to agree with your findings.
- Be brave.
- Be willing to be the pointy end of the spear.
- Be vulnerable.
- Listen.
- Be willing to go the distance.
- Don't give in to status-quo thinking.
- Don't be intimidated by your buyers, your bosses, or your teammates.

- Don't start this work thinking you already know the answer.
- Don't present your recommendations until your work is completed.
- Don't keep people in the dark on your progress—provide periodic insights and updates.
- Don't get frustrated.

Finally—and perhaps the most important thing to do as you embark on your buyer's journey—have fun with this. Be excited to be an explorer. Be happy to have this opportunity to innovate and change how you're doing business in a way that delivers a better, more remarkable experience to your customers. Be their advocate. Be their voice. Be a learner.

Acknowledgments

I have been blessed to have my life intersect with so many truly authentic, wonderful, caring, and loving individuals. These are the people who have helped me realize my passion and conduct very fulfilling and satisfying work.

At the very top of that list is my wife. She's stayed calm as I've changed companies, taken chances, and moved my family four times to four different states. She's been my sounding board, my confidante, my conscience, and my best friend. She is the most thoughtful and loving person I know, and she has always supported my work and me unconditionally. She's been there to encourage me and keep me centered. I could not have written this book without her. I love you, babe.

My two wonderful kids, Joelle and Dominic, have been such an incredible blessing and inspiration in my life. They have endured multiple moves across the country having to make new friends, start new schools, and all the while learning to adapt. I continue to be amazed at their resilience, their intelligence, and perhaps, most of all, I am in awe of the kind, generous, and loving young adults they have grown to become. I'm so proud to be their dad.

While I didn't enjoy school when I was a student, I have become a student of revenue growth and all the components necessary to deliver consistent, reliable, and predictable results. I have been blessed to have spent time with some great leaders throughout my career who helped shape, shift, and stretch my thinking. I am forever grateful for the kindness, caring, and mentoring they have provided me on this incredible journey. Thank you to Miguel de Jesus, Steve Diorio, Shawn Edgington, Gerry Guerra, Mike Hogan, Peter Lehmann, Carl Miserendino, David Morton, Neal Rohrer, Carla Vel, Marty Welch, Rob Wentling, and Peter Zink.

Moncur is a branding and digital marketing agency with offices in Detroit, Miami, and Austin, Texas. I was fortunate enough to meet David Moncur in 2010, and we have worked together transforming three different brands that have produced remarkable double-digit growth. Moncur designed the cover and layout of my book, and also did the photo shoot that produced the picture on the back cover. A special thanks to Heather Kovarik, who led the creative effort behind the cover design, along with being my wardrobe advisor, and Adam Claeys, who brought this to life with a great design concept. I can't thank each of you enough for your creative ideas and the beautiful work you delivered for this book.

A special shout out to Charlie Anderson, Christine DeRosa, Kathy Goll, Peter Lehmann and David Moncur who served as the test subjects for this book. I can't say enough how much I appreciate the time you spent reading and providing your feedback and input. Thank you.

Tom Locke, my editor at CreateSpace was instrumental in helping me shape this work. His guidance, input, and feedback was critical and allowed me to produce a better book than I could have on my own. Thanks so much Tom.

My life would not be the same without my best friend Sean Yarton. The memories we share are irreplaceable. You've been there every step of the way to make me laugh, provide perspective, and to just listen when needed. You are my brother and I have nothing but love and admiration for you.

Finally, without my mom and dad, I wouldn't be here. Of course that's an obvious statement, but what's not so obvious is the work ethic they instilled in me at an early age. They taught me the importance of doing everything to the best of my ability, even if it was something I wasn't happy doing at the time. They have encouraged me to take chances and have always been there to support my many adventures throughout my career. Thank you both so much for being great role models and believing in me. I love you dearly.

Made in the USA
Middletown, DE
09 January 2019